WEEKNIGHT COOKING

FOR BEGINNERS!

Simple, delicious and stress-free
ideas for aspiring cooks

pil

Publications International, Ltd.

Let's get social!

@Publications_International

@PublicationsInternational

www.pilbooks.com

CONTENTS

MEAL PLANNING FOR BEGINNERS

Planning meals for yourself, your family, or even for entertaining can be an overwhelming task. Let's face it, not everyone is skilled at getting a tasty, well-balanced meal on the table, especially night after night.

Whether you need to cook for one or cook for many, meal planning takes work. But, if you learn to master the process, you'll soon find that life can be stress-free, you'll save money, enjoy eating better, and you'll ultimately feel good.

HOW TO START

LOOK AT THE WEEK AHEAD

Think about what nights you and your family will be home, what meals need to be made, and how many people need to be fed.

SELECT RECIPES

Whether you choose to prepare your favorite meals, plan according to a specific theme for the day, or make a meal for a special occasion, you'll need to decide what you want to prepare this week.

MAKE A SHOPPING LIST

Review the recipes you selected, and prepare a list of ingredients you'll need to purchase.

ASSESS YOUR STAPLES

Review what staples you have on hand in the pantry, refrigerator, and freezer. Note what you need to replenish.

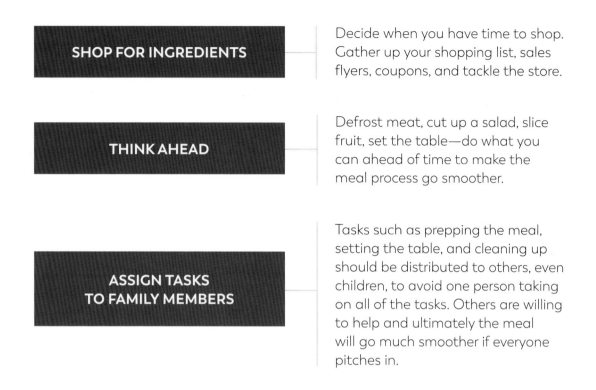

SHOP FOR INGREDIENTS

Decide when you have time to shop. Gather up your shopping list, sales flyers, coupons, and tackle the store.

THINK AHEAD

Defrost meat, cut up a salad, slice fruit, set the table—do what you can ahead of time to make the meal process go smoother.

ASSIGN TASKS TO FAMILY MEMBERS

Tasks such as prepping the meal, setting the table, and cleaning up should be distributed to others, even children, to avoid one person taking on all of the tasks. Others are willing to help and ultimately the meal will go much smoother if everyone pitches in.

WHAT IS MEAL PLANNING?

Deciding what's for dinner ahead of time, rather than looking in the refrigerator for something to "grab" on the night in question will ultimately reduce your stress and help you save time in the long run. Having a well-stocked pantry, refrigerator, and freezer with ingredients that you frequently use and planning your grocery shopping trips with a list in hand, can help you stay organized and be more efficient along the way.

Sunday is the beginning of the week and a good time to start. If you have extra time on the weekend, plan to begin your preparations then. You can also plan to prepare a larger meal with some leftovers to help out during the week if something comes up at the last minute and time does not permit you to prepare something else. For example, double your recipe for spaghetti and meatballs or lasagna so you'll have some leftovers for another meal or two during the week.

Or, think in terms of "Cook Once, Eat Twice" by cooking extra boneless chicken breasts that can be available for chicken salad, tacos, or a quick stir-fry later on.

Cook Once, Eat Twice is a term used for meals that can do "double duty." Double up on the meat mixture, use half now and half later.

FIND A THEME

Some people find it easy to identify each night of the week with a theme to help manage meals. Build on a weekly calendar with your favorite recipes.

We followed suit in our collection with this theme:

MEATLESS MONDAY — Hearty, tasty meals made without meat.

TACO TUESDAY — Whether you choose traditional tacos, casseroles, or salad, we have you covered.

ONE-POT WEDNESDAY — Dinner in one pot makes for easy prep and clean up for all.

30-MINUTE THURSDAY — From prep to table in about 30 minutes.

FAMILY FAVORITES FRIDAY — All your classic favorites just in time for the weekend.

SWEET TREATS FUN DAY — Enjoy preparing something sweet to share with your friends and family.

SLOW-COOKER SLOW DAY — Easy prep and delicious results. Bring out the slow cooker and see all that you can do with it.

If creating a theme works for you, try it for a month at a time, mix it up, get all family members involved, and see what types of fun and interesting recipes you can find. Decide what you would like to cook on each night. Determine what nights you may have more time and when you might need a quicker option.

BUILD A SHOPPING LIST

First take inventory of your pantry, refrigerator, and freezer. Try to keep basic staples on hand, as these are the ingredients you tend to use over and over again. Keep a notepad accessible to everyone at home, so you can add ingredients that you need to replenish.

Pare down your weekly shopping list to remove all those ingredients you have on hand. Review any websites or flyers from your local grocery store to include items that may be on special or on sale. (It's always good to save a little money.) Categorize your list according to the layout at the grocery store. It makes it easier to list all the produce together, all the frozen items together, and so forth.

If you find that your time this week is busier than usual, you can save time by purchasing items that may already be diced or partially prepared, like pre-packaged lettuce, shredded carrots, or cut-up fruit. You'll spend a little more money, but at least you'll have a nice variety of foods.

The beauty of planning in advance is to help reduce last-minute stress that might come if you don't have everything you need while preparing your meal. It's easy to misjudge amounts, assume you have an item that you don't, or anticipate the results when they don't come out as expected. In any case, it's always good to accommodate for such situations. The emergency substitution list (*page 10*) may come in handy if you need to adjust your plans.

STAPLES LIST*

PANTRY

- Breads, bagels, pita bread
- Beans, canned and dried
- Bread crumbs
- Soups and broth
- Tuna and salmon, canned
- Flour
- Sugar
- Fruits, canned
- Herbs and spices
- Nonstick cooking spray
- Vegetable and olive oil
- Onions
- Pasta (in a variety of shapes and sizes)
- Crackers
- Cereal and oatmeal
- Potatoes
- Sauces (pasta, barbecue, soy, teriyaki)
- Tomatoes, canned
- Vegetables, canned
- Vinegar
- Rice

REFRIGERATOR AND FREEZER

- Chicken, beef, fish fillets
- Butter
- Eggs
- Dairy products, milk, yogurt, cheese
- Fruits and vegetables, frozen and fresh
- Canned breadsticks, dough, rolls
- Condiments

This is just a guide to get you started. Your list may vary from this one.

ESSENTIAL KITCHEN TOOLS TO STOCK YOUR KITCHEN*

SMALL APPLIANCES

- Blender
- Stand mixer
- Toaster
- Slow cooker
- Microwave
- Food processor
- Coffee maker

TOOLS & GADGETS

- Measuring spoons/cups
- Knives (chef, paring, serrated, bread), knife sharpener
- Potato masher
- Vegetable peeler
- Garlic press
- Wooden spoons
- Spatulas (rubber and metal)
- Ladle
- Pot holders/oven mitts
- Cutting board
- Egg separator
- Can opener
- Rolling pin
- Ice cream scoop
- Tongs
- Colander/strainer
- Funnel
- Pizza cutter
- Pastry brush
- Meat thermometer
- Kitchen shears
- Zester
- Salt/pepper shakers

COOKWARE & BAKEWARE

- Skillet/cast iron skillet
- Grill pan
- Wok
- Saucepans
- Dutch oven
- Stock pot
- Roasting pan
- Baking sheets/cookie sheets
- Casserole dishes
- Muffin pan
- Loaf pan
- Pie pan/cake pan

This is a suggested list. You may choose less or more for your personal preference.

EMERGENCY SUBSTITUTIONS LIST*

IF YOU DON'T HAVE...	USE...
3 oz. semisweet baking chocolate	3 oz. (½ cup) semisweet chocolate morsels
1 oz. unsweetened baking chocolate	3 tbsp. unsweetened cocoa plus 1 tbsp. shortening
1 teaspoon baking powder	¼ tsp. baking soda plus ½ tsp. cream of tartar
½ cup firmly packed brown sugar	½ cup granulated sugar mixed with 2 tbsp. molasses
1 cup buttermilk	1 tbsp. lemon juice or vinegar plus milk to equal 1 cup
1 tablespoon cornstarch	2 tsp. all-purpose flour
1 whole egg	2 egg yolks plus 1 tsp. cold water
1 cup honey	1¼ cups granulated sugar plus ¼ cup water
1 tablespoon lemon juice	1 tbsp. distilled white vinegar
1 cup whole milk	1 cup skim milk plus 2 tbsp. melted butter
1 cup sour cream	1 cup plain yogurt
1 cup heavy cream (for baking, not whipping)	¾ cup whole milk plus ¼ cup butter

These substitutions may not be an identical match but will help you when you find yourself short of a particular ingredient.

REMINDERS

• A well-stocked pantry, refrigerator, and freezer with frequently used ingredients and planned grocery shopping trips with a list in hand, can help you stay organized and be more efficient.

• If there's extra time on the weekend, plan to begin your preparations then. Also, prepare larger meals with some leftovers to help out during the week in case something comes up and time does not permit you to prepare something else.

• If you find that one week is busier than usual, save time by purchasing items that may already be diced or partially prepared.

Now that you have an idea of the best way to get started with your meal planning, you can give it a try. Have fun with your process and get everyone involved. You'll soon realize what a great time saver, money saver, and stress saver meal planning can be.

MEATLESS MONDAY

TOFU "FRIED" RICE

MAKES 1 SERVING

MICROWAVE DIRECTIONS

1. Press tofu between paper towels to remove excess water. Cut into $1/2$-inch cubes.

2. Combine tofu, broccoli and edamame in large microwavable mug; mix well. Microwave on HIGH 1 minute.

3. Stir in rice, green onion, soy sauce, garlic powder, oil and sriracha, if desired. Microwave 1 minute or until heated through. Stir well before serving.

2 ounces extra firm tofu

$1/4$ cup finely chopped broccoli

$1/4$ cup thawed frozen shelled edamame

$1/3$ cup cooked brown rice

1 tablespoon chopped green onion

$1/2$ teaspoon low-sodium soy sauce

$1/8$ teaspoon garlic powder

$1/8$ teaspoon sesame oil

$1/8$ teaspoon sriracha* or hot chili sauce (optional)

*Sriracha is a Thai hot sauce that can be found in the ethnic section of major supermarkets or in Asian specialty markets.

FRESH VEGETABLE LASAGNA

MAKES 8 SERVINGS

1. Cook pasta according to package directions, omitting salt; drain. Rinse under cold running water; drain well. Set aside.

2. Preheat oven to 375°F. Combine spinach, carrots, green onions, bell pepper, parsley and black pepper in large bowl; set aside.

3. Combine cottage cheese, buttermilk, yogurt and egg whites in food processor or blender. Cover; process until smooth.

4. Spray 13×9-inch baking pan with nonstick cooking spray. Arrange one third of lasagna noodles in bottom of pan. Spread with half of cottage cheese mixture, half of vegetable mixture, half of mushrooms, half of artichokes and ³⁄₄ cup mozzarella cheese. Repeat layers, ending with noodles. Sprinkle with remaining ¹⁄₂ cup mozzarella and Parmesan cheeses.

5. Cover; bake 30 minutes. Remove cover; continue baking 20 minutes or until bubbly and heated through. Let stand 10 minutes.

- 8 ounces uncooked lasagna noodles
- 1 package (10 ounces) frozen chopped spinach, thawed and squeezed dry
- 1 cup shredded carrots
- ¹⁄₂ cup sliced green onions
- ¹⁄₂ cup sliced red bell pepper (1-inch pieces)
- ¹⁄₄ cup chopped fresh parsley
- ¹⁄₂ teaspoon black pepper
- 1¹⁄₂ cups low-fat (1%) cottage cheese
- ¹⁄₂ to 1 cup buttermilk
- ¹⁄₂ cup plain fat-free yogurt
- 2 egg whites
- 1 cup sliced mushrooms
- 1 can (14 ounces) artichoke hearts, rinsed, drained and chopped
- 2 cups (8 ounces) shredded part-skim mozzarella cheese
- ¹⁄₄ cup grated Parmesan cheese

MEATLESS SLOPPY JOES

MAKES 4 SERVINGS

1. Spray large nonstick skillet with nonstick cooking spray; heat over medium heat until hot. Add onions, bell peppers and garlic. Cook and stir 5 minutes or until vegetables are tender. Stir in ketchup and mustard.

2. Add beans, tomato sauce and chili powder. Reduce heat to medium-low. Cook 5 minutes or until thickened, stirring frequently and adding up to $1/3$ cup vinegar if dry. Serve on sandwich rolls.

2 **cups thinly sliced onions**

2 **cups chopped green bell peppers**

2 **cloves garlic, finely chopped**

2 **tablespoons ketchup**

1 **tablespoon yellow mustard**

1 **can (about 15 ounces) kidney beans, rinsed, drained and mashed**

1 **can (8 ounces) tomato sauce**

1 **teaspoon chili powder**

Cider vinegar

4 **sandwich rolls**

PENNE PASTA WITH CHUNKY TOMATO SAUCE AND SPINACH

MAKES 8 SERVINGS

1. Cook pasta according to package directions, omitting salt.

2. Meanwhile, heat marinara sauce and tomato in medium saucepan over medium heat 3 to 4 minutes or until hot and bubbly, stirring occasionally. Remove from heat; stir in spinach.

3. Drain pasta; return to saucepan. Add sauce; toss to combine. Divide evenly among 8 serving bowls; top with cheese and basil.

8 ounces uncooked multigrain penne pasta

2 cups spicy marinara sauce

1 large ripe tomato, chopped (about 1½ cups)

4 cups packed baby spinach or torn spinach leaves (4 ounces)

¼ cup grated Parmesan cheese

¼ cup chopped fresh basil

VEGETARIAN PAELLA

MAKES 6 SERVINGS

SLOW COOKER DIRECTIONS

1. Heat oil in small nonstick skillet over medium-high heat. Add onion; cook and stir 6 to 7 minutes or until tender. Stir in garlic. Transfer to slow cooker. Stir in rice.

2. Add broth, tomatoes, zucchini, bell pepper, Italian seasoning, turmeric and ground red pepper; mix well. Cover; cook on LOW 4 hours or on HIGH 2 hours or until liquid is absorbed.

3. Stir in artichokes, peas and salt, if desired. Cover; cook on LOW 5 to 10 minutes or until vegetables are tender.

2 teaspoons canola oil

1 cup chopped onion

2 cloves garlic, minced

1 cup uncooked brown rice

2$\frac{1}{4}$ cups vegetable broth

1 can (about 14 ounces) no-salt-added stewed tomatoes

1 small zucchini, halved lengthwise and sliced to $\frac{1}{2}$-inch thickness (about 1$\frac{1}{4}$ cups)

1 cup chopped red bell pepper

2 teaspoons Italian seasoning

$\frac{1}{2}$ teaspoon ground turmeric

$\frac{1}{8}$ teaspoon ground red pepper

1 can (14 ounces) quartered artichoke hearts, drained

$\frac{1}{2}$ cup frozen baby peas

$\frac{3}{4}$ teaspoon salt (optional)

ZITI RATATOUILLE

MAKES 6 TO 8 SERVINGS

SLOW COOKER DIRECTIONS

1. Layer eggplant, zucchini, bell pepper, onion, garlic, marinara sauce and tomatoes in slow cooker. Cover; cook on LOW 4$\frac{1}{2}$ hours.

2. Stir in pasta and olives. Cover; cook on LOW 25 minutes or until pasta is tender. Drizzle with lemon juice and sprinkle with Parmesan cheese, if desired.

1 large eggplant, peeled and cut into $\frac{1}{2}$-inch cubes (about 1$\frac{1}{2}$ pounds)

2 medium zucchini, cut into $\frac{1}{2}$-inch cubes

1 green or red bell pepper, cut into $\frac{1}{2}$-inch pieces

1 onion, chopped

4 cloves garlic, minced

1 jar (about 24 ounces) marinara sauce

2 cans (about 14 ounces each) diced tomatoes with garlic and onions

8 ounces uncooked ziti pasta

1 can (6 ounces) pitted black olives, drained

Lemon juice (optional)

Shaved Parmesan cheese (optional)

VEGETARIAN ORZO & FETA BAKE

MAKES 6 SERVINGS

1. Preheat oven to 450°F.

2. Combine orzo, olives and garlic in medium bowl. Place orzo mixture in center of foil sheet. Fold sides of foil up around orzo mixture, but do not seal.

3. In same bowl, combine tomatoes with juice, broth and oil. Pour over orzo mixture. Top with cheese.

4. Double fold sides and ends of foil to seal packet, leaving head space for heat circulation. Place packet on baking sheet.

5. Bake 22 to 24 minutes or until pasta is tender. Remove from oven; let stand 5 minutes. Open packet and transfer contents to serving plates.

1 package (16 ounces) uncooked orzo pasta

1 can ($4\frac{1}{4}$ ounces) chopped black olives, drained

2 cloves garlic, minced

1 sheet (24×18 inches) heavy-duty foil, lightly sprayed with nonstick cooking spray

1 can (about 14 ounces) diced Italian-style tomatoes, undrained

1 can (14 ounces) vegetable broth

2 tablespoons olive oil

6 to 8 ounces feta cheese, cut into $\frac{1}{2}$-inch cubes

LENTIL AND ORZO PASTA SALAD

MAKES 4 SERVINGS

1. Bring water to boil in Dutch oven over high heat. Add lentils; boil 12 minutes.

2. Add orzo. Cook 10 minutes or just until tender; drain. Rinse under cold running water to cool completely; drain well.

3. Meanwhile, combine remaining ingredients except feta in large bowl; set aside.

4. Add lentil mixture to tomato mixture; toss gently to blend. Add feta; toss gently. Let stand 15 minutes before serving.

- 8 cups water
- 1/2 cup dried lentils, rinsed and sorted
- 4 ounces uncooked orzo
- 1 1/2 cups quartered cherry tomatoes, sweet grape variety
- 3/4 cup finely chopped celery
- 1/2 cup chopped red onion
- 2 ounces pitted olives (about 16 olives), coarsely chopped
- 3 to 4 tablespoons cider vinegar
- 1 tablespoon olive oil
- 1 tablespoon dried basil
- 1 medium clove garlic, minced
- 1/8 teaspoon red pepper flakes
- 4 ounces feta cheese with sun-dried tomatoes and basil

VEGGIE PIZZA PITAS
MAKES 4 SERVINGS

1. Preheat oven to 475°F.

2. Arrange pita rounds, rough sides up, in single layer on large nonstick baking sheet. Spread 1 tablespoon pizza sauce evenly over each round to within 1/4 inch of edge. Sprinkle with basil and red pepper flakes, if desired. Top with mushrooms, bell pepper and onion. Sprinkle with mozzarella cheese.

3. Bake 5 minutes or until mozzarella cheese is melted. Sprinkle 1/2 teaspoon Parmesan cheese over each round.

2 whole wheat pita bread rounds, cut in half horizontally (to make 4 rounds)

1/4 cup pizza sauce

1 teaspoon dried basil

1/8 teaspoon red pepper flakes (optional)

1 cup sliced mushrooms

1/2 cup thinly sliced green bell pepper

1/2 cup thinly sliced red onion

1 cup (4 ounces) shredded part-skim mozzarella cheese

2 teaspoons grated Parmesan cheese

BLACK BEAN CHILI

MAKES 6 SERVINGS

1. Sort beans, discarding any foreign material. Place beans in 8-quart Dutch oven. Add enough cold water to cover beans by 2 inches. Cover; bring to a boil over high heat. Boil 2 minutes. Remove from heat; let soak, covered, 1 hour. Drain. Add 6 cups water and bay leaf to beans in Dutch oven. Return to heat. Bring to a boil. Reduce heat and simmer, partially covered, 1 to 2 hours or until tender.

2. Meanwhile, heat oil in large skillet over medium heat. Add onions and garlic; cook until onions are tender. Coarsely chop tomatoes; add to skillet. Add jalapeño peppers, chili powder, salt, paprika, oregano, cocoa, cumin and cinnamon. Simmer 15 minutes. Add tomato mixture to beans. Stir in vinegar. Continue simmering 30 minutes or until beans are very tender and chili has thickened slightly. Remove and discard bay leaf. Ladle chili into individual bowls. Serve with condiments.

1 pound uncooked dried black beans

Cold water

6 cups water

1 whole bay leaf

3 tablespoons vegetable oil

2 large onions, chopped

3 cloves garlic, minced

1 can (about 14 ounces) diced tomatoes

2 to 3 fresh or canned jalapeño peppers,* stemmed, seeded and minced

2 tablespoons chili powder

1½ teaspoons salt

1 teaspoon paprika

1 teaspoon dried oregano

1 teaspoon unsweetened cocoa powder

½ teaspoon ground cumin

¼ teaspoon ground cinnamon

1 tablespoon red wine vinegar

CONDIMENTS (OPTIONAL)

1 cup plain yogurt or sour cream

Picante sauce

½ cup sliced green onions or chopped fresh cilantro

Jalapeño peppers can sting and irritate the skin, so wear rubber gloves when handling peppers and do not touch your eyes.

VEGETARIAN RICE NOODLES

MAKES 4 SERVINGS

1. Combine soy sauce, sugar, lime juice and chiles in small bowl until well blended; set aside.

2. Place rice noodles in medium bowl. Cover with hot water; let stand 15 minutes or until soft. Drain well; cut into 3-inch lengths.

3. Meanwhile, heat oil in large skillet over medium-high heat. Add tofu; stir-fry 4 minutes per side or until golden brown. Remove with slotted spatula to paper towel-lined baking sheet.

4. Add jicama to skillet; stir-fry 5 minutes or until lightly browned. Remove to baking sheet. Stir-fry sweet potatoes in batches until tender and browned; remove to baking sheet. Add leeks; stir-fry 1 minute; remove to baking sheet.

5. Stir soy sauce mixture; add to skillet. Heat until sugar dissolves. Add noodles; toss to coat. Gently stir in tofu, vegetables, peanuts, mint and cilantro.

$1/2$ cup soy sauce

$1/3$ cup sugar

$1/4$ cup lime juice

2 fresh red Thai chiles *or* 1 large jalapeño pepper,* finely chopped

8 ounces thin rice noodles (rice vermicelli)

$1/4$ cup vegetable oil

8 ounces firm tofu, drained and cut into triangles

1 jicama (8 ounces), peeled and chopped *or* 1 can (8 ounces) sliced water chestnuts, drained

2 medium sweet potatoes (1 pound), peeled and cut into $1/4$-inch-thick slices

2 large leeks, cut into $1/4$-inch-thick slices

$1/4$ cup chopped unsalted dry-roasted peanuts

2 tablespoons chopped fresh mint

2 tablespoons chopped fresh cilantro

*Chile peppers can sting and irritate the skin, so wear rubber gloves when handling peppers and do not touch your eyes.

QUINOA BURRITO BOWLS
MAKES 4 SERVINGS

1. Place quinoa in fine-mesh strainer; rinse well under cold running water. Bring 2 cups water to a boil in small saucepan; stir in quinoa. Reduce heat to low; cover and simmer 10 to 15 minutes or until quinoa is tender and water is absorbed. Stir in 1 tablespoon lime juice. Cover and keep warm. Combine sour cream and remaining 1 tablespoon lime juice in small bowl; set aside.

2. Meanwhile, heat oil in large skillet over medium heat. Add onion and bell pepper; cook and stir 5 minutes or until softened. Add garlic; cook 1 minute. Add black beans and corn; cook 3 to 5 minutes or until heated through.

3. Divide quinoa among 4 serving bowls; top with black bean mixture, lettuce and sour cream mixture. Garnish with lime wedges.

- 1 cup uncooked quinoa
- 2 cups water
- 2 tablespoons fresh lime juice, divided
- ¼ cup light sour cream
- 2 teaspoons vegetable oil
- 1 small onion, diced
- 1 red bell pepper, diced
- 1 clove garlic, minced
- ½ cup canned black beans, rinsed and drained
- ½ cup thawed frozen corn
- Shredded lettuce
- Lime wedges (optional)

VEGETARIAN QUINOA CHILI
MAKES 4 TO 6 SERVINGS

1. Heat oil over medium-high heat in large saucepan. Add onion, bell pepper, carrot and celery; cook about 10 minutes or until vegetables are softened, stirring occasionally. Add jalapeño pepper, garlic, chili powder, cumin and salt, if desired; cook about 1 minute or until fragrant.

2. Add beans, tomatoes, water, corn and quinoa; bring to a boil. Reduce heat to low; cover and simmer 1 hour, stirring occasionally.

3. Spoon into bowls; garnish with toppings as desired.

- 2 tablespoons vegetable oil
- 1 large onion
- 1 red bell pepper, diced
- 1 large carrot, peeled and diced
- 1 stalk celery, diced
- 1 jalapeño pepper*, seeded and finely chopped
- 1 tablespoon minced garlic
- 3 tablespoons chili powder
- 2 teaspoons ground cumin
- 1 teaspoon kosher salt (optional)
- 1 can (about 15 ounces) kidney beans, rinsed and drained
- 1 can (28 ounces) crushed tomatoes
- 1 cup water
- 1 cup fresh or frozen corn
- 1/2 cup uncooked quinoa, rinsed well

Optional toppings: diced avocado, shredded Cheddar cheese and sliced green onions

*Jalapeño peppers can sting and irritate the skin, so wear rubber gloves when handling peppers and do not touch your eyes.

HEARTY VEGETARIAN MAC AND CHEESE

MAKES 6 SERVINGS

SLOW COOKER DIRECTIONS

1. Coat inside of slow cooker with nonstick cooking spray. Add tomatoes, Alfredo sauce, 1 cup mozzarella cheese, pasta, sausage, 1/2 cup basil, broth and salt to slow cooker; stir to blend. Top with remaining 1/2 cup mozzarella cheese and Parmesan cheese.

2. Cover; cook on LOW 3 1/2 hours or on HIGH 2 hours. Top with remaining 1/4 cup basil.

1 can (about 14 ounces) stewed tomatoes, undrained

1 1/2 cups prepared Alfredo sauce

1 1/2 cups (6 ounces) shredded mozzarella cheese, divided

8 ounces whole grain pasta (medium shells or penne shape), cooked and drained

7 ounces Italian-flavored vegetarian sausage links, cut into 1/4-inch slices

3/4 cup fresh basil leaves, thinly sliced and divided

1/2 cup vegetable broth

1/2 teaspoon salt

2 tablespoons grated Parmesan cheese

TACO TUESDAY

FESTIVE TACO CUPS
MAKES 24 TACO CUPS

1. Heat oil in large skillet over medium heat. Add onion; cook until tender. Add turkey; cook and stir until turkey is no longer pink. Stir in garlic, oregano, chili powder and salt. Remove from heat and stir in $1/2$ cup cheese; set aside.

2. Preheat oven to 375°F. Lightly grease 24 mini ($1^3/_4$-inch) muffin cups. Remove dough from container but do not unroll dough. Separate dough into 8 pieces at perforations. Divide each piece into 3 pieces; roll or pat each piece into 3-inch circle. Press circles into prepared muffin cups.

3. Fill each cup with $1^1/_2$ to 2 teaspoons turkey mixture. Bake 10 minutes. Sprinkle tops of taco cups with remaining $3/4$ cup cheese; bake 2 to 3 minutes or until cheese is melted. Garnish with tomato and green onion.

1 tablespoon vegetable oil

$1/2$ cup chopped onion

$1/2$ pound ground turkey or ground beef

1 clove garlic, minced

$1/2$ teaspoon dried oregano

$1/2$ teaspoon chili powder or taco seasoning mix

$1/4$ teaspoon salt

$1^1/_4$ cups (5 ounces) shredded taco cheese or Mexican cheese blend, divided

1 can ($11^1/_2$ ounces) refrigerated breadstick dough

Chopped fresh tomato and sliced green onion (optional)

LAYERED TACO SALAD

MAKES 4 SERVINGS

1. Spray medium nonstick skillet with nonstick cooking spray; heat over medium-high heat. Brown beef 3 to 5 minutes, stirring to break up meat. Drain fat. Stir in chili powder and 1 teaspoon cumin. Let cool.

2. Combine picante sauce, sugar and remaining ½ teaspoon cumin in small bowl.

3. Place lettuce in 11×7-inch casserole. Layer with beef, tomatoes, green onions, cilantro and chips. Top with sour cream; sprinkle with cheese. Spoon picante sauce mixture on top.

½ **pound ground beef**

1½ **teaspoons chili powder**

1½ **teaspoons ground cumin, divided**

½ **cup picante sauce**

1 **teaspoon sugar**

6 **cups shredded romaine lettuce**

2 **plum tomatoes, seeded and diced**

½ **cup chopped green onions**

¼ **cup chopped fresh cilantro**

28 **tortilla chips, crumbled (2 ounces)**

½ **cup sour cream**

½ **cup (2 ounces) shredded sharp Cheddar cheese or Mexican cheese blend**

TACO POT PIE

MAKES 4 TO 6 SERVINGS

1. Preheat oven to 400°F. Brown beef in medium ovenproof skillet over medium-high heat 6 to 8 minutes, stirring to break up meat. Drain fat. Add taco seasoning mix and water to skillet. Cook over medium-low heat 3 minutes or until most liquid is absorbed, stirring occasionally.

2. Stir in beans, tomatoes, corn and peas. Cook 3 minutes or until mixture is heated through. Remove from heat; stir in cheese.

3. Unwrap breadstick dough; separate into strips. Twist strips, cutting to fit skillet.* Arrange attractively over meat mixture. Press ends of dough lightly to edge of skillet to secure. Bake 15 minutes or until bread is golden brown and meat mixture is bubbly.

You can also transfer mixture into 13×9-inch casserole dish and top with breadsticks before baking.

1 pound ground beef

1 package (about 1 ounce) taco seasoning mix

$1/4$ cup water

1 cup canned kidney beans, rinsed and drained

1 cup chopped tomatoes

$3/4$ cup frozen corn, thawed

$3/4$ cup frozen peas, thawed

$1^1/2$ cups (6 ounces) shredded Cheddar cheese

1 can ($11^1/2$ ounces) refrigerated breadstick dough

RAMEN "SPAGHETTI" TACOS

MAKES 4 SERVINGS

1. Prepare noodles according to package directions. Drain well; return to saucepan. Add pasta sauce. Cook over medium heat until heated through.

2. Divide noodles evenly among taco shells. Top each taco with mozzarella and Cheddar cheeses. Microwave on HIGH at 10- to 15-second intervals until cheeses are melted, if desired. Top with tomatoes.

TIP: These tacos can be flavored in a variety of ways. Try them with salsa instead of pasta sauce and toppings such as sour cream, guacamole, shredded lettuce and grated Mexican cheese. Or, mix cooked noodles with teriyaki sauce and top with shredded cabbage, water chestnuts, bamboo shoots and chicken or pork.

2 packages (3 ounces each) ramen noodles, any flavor*

1 cup pasta sauce

8 hard taco shells

1/2 cup grated mozzarella cheese

1/4 cup (2 ounces) shredded Cheddar cheese

Chopped fresh tomatoes

Discard seasoning packets.

SPICY BEEF TACOS

MAKES 6 SERVINGS

1. Brown beef in 2 tablespoons hot oil in large skillet over medium-high heat 10 to 12 minutes, turning frequently. Reduce heat to low. Stir in chili powder, garlic, salt and cumin. Cook and stir 30 seconds.

2. Add diced tomatoes with juice. Bring to a boil over high heat. Reduce heat to low. Cover and simmer 1½ to 2 hours or until beef is very tender.

3. Using two forks, pull beef into coarse shreds in skillet. Increase heat to medium. Cook, uncovered, 10 to 15 minutes or until most of liquid has evaporated. Keep warm.

4. Heat 4 to 5 inches of oil in deep fat fryer or deep saucepan over medium-high heat to 375°F; adjust heat to maintain temperature.

5. For taco shells, place 1 tortilla in taco fryer basket;** close gently. Fry tortilla 30 seconds to 1 minute until crisp and golden. Open basket; gently remove taco shell. Drain on paper towels. Repeat with remaining tortillas.

6. Fill taco shells with beef, cheese, lettuce and chopped tomato. Garnish with cilantro, if desired.

**Taco fryer baskets are available in large supermarkets and in household stores.

1 pound boneless beef chuck, cut into 1-inch cubes

Vegetable oil

1 to 2 teaspoons chili powder

1 clove garlic, minced

½ teaspoon salt

½ teaspoon ground cumin

1 can (about 14 ounces) diced tomatoes, undrained

12 (6-inch) corn tortillas*

1 cup (4 ounces) shredded mild Cheddar cheese

2 to 3 cups shredded iceberg lettuce

1 large fresh tomato, seeded and chopped

Chopped fresh cilantro (optional)

*Or, substitute packaged taco shells for the corn tortillas. Omit steps 4 and 5. Warm taco shells according to package directions.

TACO SALAD CASSEROLE

MAKES 6 TO 8 SERVINGS

1. Preheat oven to 350°F.

2. Cook and stir beef and onion in large skillet over medium heat until beef is no longer pink, stirring to break up meat. Drain fat. Add chili with beans, tomatoes, green chiles and taco seasoning mix; cook and stir until heated through.

3. Place half of crushed tortilla chips in 2½-quart casserole. Pour meat mixture over chips; top with cheeses and remaining chips.

4. Bake 30 to 40 minutes or until hot and bubbly. Serve over lettuce; top with taco sauce and sour cream.

1 pound ground beef

1 cup chopped onion

1 can (15 ounces) chili with beans

1 can (about 14 ounces) diced tomatoes

1 can (4 ounces) diced mild green chiles

1 package (about 1 ounce) taco seasoning mix

1 bag (12 ounces) nacho-flavored tortilla chips, crushed

2 cups (8 ounces) shredded Cheddar cheese

2 cups (8 ounces) shredded mozzarella cheese

3 to 4 cups shredded lettuce

1 jar (8 ounces) prepared taco sauce

½ cup sour cream

TACO PIZZA

MAKES 4 SERVINGS

1. Preheat oven to 425°F. Lightly spray 12-inch pizza pan with nonstick cooking spray. Unroll pizza dough; press into prepared pan. Build up edges slightly. Prick dough with fork. Bake 7 to 10 minutes or until lightly browned.

2. Meanwhile, lightly spray large nonstick skillet with cooking spray. Add ground turkey and onion; cook and stir until turkey is no longer pink. Add tomato sauce and taco seasoning mix; bring to a boil. Reduce heat; simmer, uncovered, 2 to 3 minutes. Spoon turkey mixture on warm pizza crust. Bake 5 minutes.

3. Arrange tomatoes over turkey mixture. Sprinkle with cheese. Bake 2 to 3 minutes or until cheese melts. Top with lettuce. Cut into 8 pieces before serving.

1 package (about 14 ounces) refrigerated pizza dough

¾ pound ground turkey

½ cup chopped onion

1 can (8 ounces) tomato sauce

1 package (about 1 ounce) taco seasoning mix

2 medium plum tomatoes, thinly sliced, *or* 1 cup chopped tomato

1 cup (4 ounces) shredded Cheddar cheese

1½ cups shredded lettuce

DEVIL'S FIRE SHREDDED BEEF TACOS

MAKES 6 TO 8 SERVINGS

SLOW COOKER DIRECTIONS

1. Season beef with 1 teaspoon salt, cumin, garlic powder and smoked paprika. Heat 1 tablespoon oil in large skillet over medium-high heat. Add beef; cook 5 minutes on each side until browned. Remove to slow cooker.

2. Pour in broth. Cover; cook on LOW 8 to 9 hours or on HIGH 4 to 5 hours.

3. Meanwhile, preheat oven to 425°F. Combine bell pepper, tomato, onion and garlic on large baking sheet. Drizzle with remaining 1 tablespoon oil. Roast 40 minutes or until vegetables are tender. Place vegetables, chipotle pepper, lime juice and remaining 1/4 teaspoon salt in food processor or blender; blend until smooth.

4. Remove beef to large cutting board; shred with 2 forks. Combine shredded meat with 1 cup cooking liquid. Discard remaining cooking liquid. Serve on tortillas with sauce. Top as desired.

1 boneless beef chuck roast (2½ pounds)

1¼ teaspoons salt, divided

1 teaspoon *each* ground cumin, garlic powder and smoked paprika

2 tablespoons olive oil, divided

2 cups beef broth

1 red bell pepper, sliced

1 tomato, cut into wedges

½ onion, sliced

2 cloves garlic, minced

1 to 2 canned chipotle peppers in adobo sauce

Juice of 1 lime

Corn or flour tortillas

Optional toppings: sliced bell peppers, avocado, diced onion, lime wedges and/or chopped fresh cilantro

TAKE A TACO SALAD TO WORK

MAKES 4 (1-QUART) JARS

1. For dressing, whisk mayonnaise, yogurt, 1 tablespoon lime juice, chili powder and garlic in small bowl. Stir in cheese and cilantro.

2. For salad, heat oil in saucepan over high heat. Add corn; cook 10 to 15 minutes or until lightly browned, stirring occasionally. Stir in salt. Transfer to medium bowl; cool to room temperature. Combine avocado and 1 teaspoon lime juice in small bowl; toss to coat.

3. For each 1-quart jar, layer 2½ tablespoons dressing, ½ cup corn, scant ½ cup black beans, ¼ cup tomatoes, 2 tablespoons red onion and about ¼ cup avocado. Top with tortilla strips and lettuce. Seal jars.

4. Refrigerate until ready to serve.

NOTE: You can also make these without the lettuce. If so, use 4 (1-pint) jars.

DRESSING

¼ cup mayonnaise

¼ cup plain yogurt or sour cream

1 tablespoon lime juice

½ teaspoon chipotle chili powder

1 clove garlic, minced

¼ cup crumbled cotija cheese

¼ cup chopped fresh cilantro

SALAD

1 tablespoon vegetable oil

1 package (16 ounces) frozen corn

¼ teaspoon salt

1 large avocado, diced

1 teaspoon lime juice

1 can (about 15 ounces) black beans, rinsed and drained

2 medium tomatoes, seeded and diced (1 cup)

½ cup finely chopped red onion

Packaged tortilla strips or chips

Chopped fresh lettuce or spinach

TACO SALAD SUPREME
MAKES 4 SERVINGS

1. Combine beef, onion and celery in large saucepan; cook over medium-high heat 6 to 8 minutes or until beef is no longer pink, stirring to break up meat. Drain fat.

2. Add chopped tomatoes, jalapeño pepper, chili powder, salt, cumin and black pepper; cook and stir 1 minute. Stir in tomato sauce, beans and 1 cup water; bring to a boil. Reduce heat to medium-low; cook about 1 hour or until most of liquid is absorbed.

3. For each salad, combine 2 cups lettuce and ½ cup diced tomatoes in individual bowls. Top with 12 tortilla chips, ¾ cup chili, ¼ cup salsa and 2 tablespoons sour cream. Sprinkle with ¼ cup cheese. (Reserve remaining chili for another use.)

CHILI
- 1 pound ground beef
- 1 medium onion, chopped
- 1 stalk celery, chopped
- 2 medium fresh tomatoes, chopped
- 1 jalapeño pepper,* finely chopped
- 1½ teaspoons chili powder
- 1 teaspoon salt
- 1 teaspoon ground cumin
- ½ teaspoon black pepper
- 1 can (15 ounces) tomato sauce
- 1 can (about 15 ounces) kidney beans, rinsed and drained
- 1 can (about 15 ounces) pinto beans, rinsed and drained

SALAD
- 8 cups chopped romaine lettuce (large pieces)
- 2 cups diced fresh tomatoes
- 48 small round tortilla chips
- 1 cup salsa
- ½ cup sour cream
- 1 cup (4 ounces) shredded Cheddar cheese

*Jalapeño peppers can sting and irritate the skin, so wear rubber gloves when handling peppers and do not touch your eyes.

ISLAND FISH TACOS
MAKES 4 SERVINGS

1. For coleslaw, combine jicama, coleslaw mix and 3 tablespoons cilantro in medium bowl. Whisk ¼ cup lime juice, ¼ cup oil, vinegar, mayonnaise, honey and 1 teaspoon salt in small bowl until well blended. Pour over vegetable mixture; stir to coat. Let stand at least 15 minutes for flavors to blend.

2. For salsa, place tomatoes in fine-mesh strainer; set in bowl or sink to drain 15 minutes Transfer to another medium bowl. Stir in onion, ¼ cup cilantro, 2 tablespoons lime juice, jalapeño pepper and 1 teaspoon salt; mix well.

3. For tacos, season both sides of fish with salt and black pepper. Heat 1 tablespoon oil in large nonstick skillet over medium-high heat. Add half of fish; cook about 2 minutes per side or until fish is opaque and begins to flake when tested with fork. Repeat with remaining oil and fish.

4. Serve fish in tortillas with coleslaw and salsa. Serve with guacamole, if desired.

COLESLAW
- 1 medium jicama (about 12 ounces), peeled and shredded
- 2 cups shredded coleslaw mix
- 3 tablespoons finely chopped fresh cilantro
- ¼ cup lime juice
- ¼ cup vegetable oil
- 3 tablespoons white vinegar
- 2 tablespoons mayonnaise
- 1 tablespoon honey
- 1 teaspoon salt

SALSA
- 2 medium fresh tomatoes, diced (about 2 cups)
- ½ cup finely chopped red onion
- ¼ cup finely chopped fresh cilantro
- 2 tablespoons lime juice
- 2 tablespoons minced jalapeño pepper
- 1 teaspoon salt

TACOS
- 1 to 1¼ pounds white fish such as tilapia or mahi mahi, cut into 3×1½-inch pieces
- Salt and black pepper
- 2 tablespoons vegetable oil
- 12 (6-inch) taco-size tortillas, heated
- Prepared guacamole (optional)

MINI CARNITAS TACOS

MAKES 12 SERVINGS (36 MINI TACOS)

SLOW COOKER DIRECTIONS

1. Combine pork, onion, broth, chili powder, cumin, oregano and chipotle pepper, if desired, in slow cooker. Cover; cook on LOW 6 hours or on HIGH 3 hours or until pork is very tender. Pour off excess cooking liquid.

2. Shred pork with 2 forks; stir in pico de gallo, cilantro and salt. Cover and keep warm.

3. Cut 3 circles from each tortilla with 2-inch biscuit cutter. Top with pork, cheese and sour cream.

TIP: Carnitas means "little meats" in Spanish. This dish is usually made with an inexpensive cut of pork that is simmered for a long time until it falls to pieces. The meat is then browned in pork fat. The slow cooker makes the long, slow cooking process easy to manage and skipping the final browning lowers the fat content.

$1\frac{1}{2}$ pounds boneless pork loin, cut into 1-inch cubes

1 onion, finely chopped

$\frac{1}{2}$ cup reduced-sodium chicken broth

1 tablespoon chili powder

2 teaspoons ground cumin

1 teaspoon dried oregano

$\frac{1}{2}$ teaspoon minced canned chipotle pepper in adobo sauce (optional)

$\frac{1}{2}$ cup pico de gallo

2 tablespoons chopped fresh cilantro

$\frac{1}{2}$ teaspoon salt

12 (6-inch) corn tortillas

$\frac{3}{4}$ cup (3 ounces) shredded sharp Cheddar cheese

3 tablespoons sour cream

FISHIN' FOR TACOS

MAKES 4 SERVINGS

1. Bake fish sticks according to package directions.

2. Mix salsa and mayonnaise in small bowl.

3. Place 3 fish sticks in each tortilla. Top evenly with salsa mixture, lettuce, cheese and tomatoes. Roll up tortillas. Serve immediately.

12 frozen fish sticks (8 ounces total)

3 tablespoons salsa

2 tablespoons mayonnaise

4 (8-inch) flour tortillas, warmed

1 cup shredded lettuce

½ cup (2 ounces) shredded Cheddar cheese

⅓ cup grape tomatoes, quartered

PORK TACOS WITH FRESH SALSA

MAKES 10 SERVINGS

SLOW COOKER DIRECTIONS

1. Combine flour, salt and black pepper in large resealable food storage bag. Add pork; shake to coat. Heat oil in large skillet over medium heat. Add pork and garlic; cook and stir 6 to 8 minutes or until pork is browned. Remove pork mixture to slow cooker using slotted spoon.

2. Add broth to skillet, stirring to scrape up any browned bits from bottom of skillet. Pour broth into slow cooker. Add bell pepper, zucchini and onion slices. Cover; cook on LOW 7 to 8 hours.

3. Meanwhile, combine tomatoes, chopped onion, jalapeño pepper, cilantro, lime juice, salt and black pepper in small bowl; stir to blend. Refrigerate until ready to use.

4. To serve tacos, place pork mixture evenly in tortillas. Serve with salsa.

TACOS

- 1/4 cup all-purpose flour
  Salt and black pepper
- 1 pound pork shoulder roast, cubed
- 1 tablespoon vegetable oil
- 2 cloves garlic, minced
- 1 cup chicken broth
- 1 large red bell pepper, sliced into strips
- 1 medium zucchini, sliced and cut into fourths
- 1 large onion, sliced

SALSA

- 3 medium plum tomatoes, chopped
- 2 tablespoons chopped onion
- 1 small jalapeño pepper, seeded and minced*
- 1 tablespoon chopped fresh cilantro
- 1 tablespoon lime juice
  Salt and black pepper
- 10 (6-inch) flour tortillas, warmed

*Jalapeño peppers can sting and irritate the skin, so wear rubber gloves when handling peppers and do not touch your eyes.

ONE-POT WEDNESDAY

FORTY-CLOVE CHICKEN FILICE

MAKES 4 TO 6 SERVINGS

1. Preheat oven to 375°F.

2. Heat oil in Dutch oven. Add chicken; cook until browned on all sides.

3. Combine garlic, celery, wine, vermouth, lemon juice, parsley, basil, oregano and red pepper flakes in medium bowl; pour over chicken. Sprinkle with lemon peel; season with salt and black pepper.

4. Cover and bake 40 minutes. Remove cover; bake 15 minutes or until chicken is cooked through (165°F).

- ¼ cup olive oil
- 1 cut-up whole chicken (about 3 pounds)
- 40 cloves garlic (about 2 heads), peeled
- 4 stalks celery, thickly sliced
- ½ cup dry white wine
- ¼ cup dry vermouth
-   Grated peel and juice of 1 lemon
- 2 tablespoons finely chopped fresh parsley
- 2 teaspoons dried basil
- 1 teaspoon dried oregano, crushed
-   Pinch red pepper flakes
-   Salt and black pepper

BROCCOLI AND BEEF PASTA

MAKES 4 SERVINGS

1. Brown beef and garlic in Dutch oven over medium-high heat 6 to 8 minutes, stirring to break up meat. Drain fat. Place meat in large bowl; set aside.

2. Add broth, onion, pasta, basil, oregano and thyme to Dutch oven. Bring to a boil; boil 10 minutes. Stir in tomatoes with juice and broccoli. Reduce heat to medium-high and simmer, uncovered, 6 to 8 minutes, stirring occasionally, until broccoli is crisp-tender and pasta is tender. Return meat to Dutch oven; simmer 3 to 4 minutes or until heated through.

3. Transfer to serving platter with slotted spoon. Sprinkle with cheese. Cover with lid or tent with foil until cheese is melted. Meanwhile, bring liquid left in Dutch oven to a boil over high heat. Boil until thick and reduced to 3 to 4 tablespoons. Spoon over pasta mixture.

SERVING SUGGESTION: Serve with garlic bread.

1 pound ground beef

2 cloves garlic, minced

1 can (about 14 ounces) beef broth

1 medium onion, thinly sliced

1 cup uncooked rotini pasta

½ teaspoon dried basil

½ teaspoon dried oregano

½ teaspoon dried thyme

1 can (about 14 ounces) Italian-style diced tomatoes

2 cups broccoli florets *or* 1 package (10 ounces) frozen broccoli, thawed

¾ cup (3 ounces) shredded Cheddar cheese or grated Parmesan cheese

HAM & CHEDDAR FRITTATA

MAKES 4 SERVINGS

1. Preheat broiler.

2. Beat eggs, egg whites, salt and black pepper in large bowl until blended. Stir in broccoli, ham and bell peppers.

3. Melt butter over medium heat in 10-inch ovenproof skillet with sloping side. Pour egg mixture into skillet; cover. Cook 5 to 6 minutes or until eggs are set around edge. (Center will be wet.)

4. Uncover; sprinkle cheese over frittata. Transfer skillet to broiler; broil, 5 inches from heat, 2 minutes or until eggs are set in center and cheese is melted. Let stand 5 minutes; cut into 4 wedges.

3 eggs

3 egg whites

$\frac{1}{2}$ teaspoon salt

$\frac{1}{2}$ teaspoon freshly ground black pepper

$1\frac{1}{2}$ cups (4 ounces) frozen broccoli florets, thawed

6 ounces deli smoked ham, cut into $\frac{1}{2}$-inch cubes ($1\frac{1}{4}$ cups)

$\frac{1}{3}$ cup drained bottled roasted red bell peppers, cut into thin strips

1 tablespoon butter

$\frac{1}{2}$ cup (2 ounces) shredded sharp Cheddar cheese

BEEF STEW
MAKES 8 SERVINGS

1. Heat oil in Dutch oven over medium-high heat. Add half of beef; sprinkle with salt and pepper. Cook about 8 minutes or until browned on all sides. Remove to bowl; repeat with remaining beef.

2. Add onions; cook and stir over medium heat about 10 minutes. Stir in carrots, mushrooms, ham and garlic; cook and stir 10 minutes or until vegetables are softened, scraping up any browned bits from bottom of Dutch oven.

3. Return beef to Dutch oven and pour in stout and broth. (Liquid should just cover beef and vegetables; add water if needed.) Stir in sugar, herbes de Provence and Worcestershire sauce; bring to a boil. Reduce heat to low; cover and simmer 2 hours or until beef is fork-tender.

4. Skim fat. Stir water into cornstarch in small bowl until smooth. Stir into stew; simmer 5 minutes. Stir in parsley. Serve over noodles.

2 tablespoons olive or vegetable oil

3 pounds boneless beef chuck, trimmed and cut into 2-inch chunks

2 teaspoons salt

1/2 teaspoon black pepper

3 medium sweet or yellow onions, halved and sliced

6 medium carrots, cut into 1/2-inch pieces

8 ounces sliced mushrooms

1/4 pound smoked ham, cut into 1/4-inch pieces

2 tablespoons minced garlic

1 can (about 15 ounces) stout

1 can (about 14 ounces) beef broth

1 teaspoon sugar

1 teaspoon herbes de Provence or dried thyme

1 teaspoon Worcestershire sauce

1/3 cup cold water

2 tablespoons cornstarch

3 tablespoons chopped fresh parsley

Hot cooked wide noodles or steamed red potatoes (optional)

PORK CHOPS AND STUFFING SKILLET CASSEROLE

MAKES 4 SERVINGS

1. Preheat oven to 350°F. Sprinkle 1 side of pork chops with thyme, paprika and salt. Spray large ovenproof skillet with nonstick cooking spray; heat over medium-high heat. Add pork, seasoned side down; cook 2 minutes. Remove to plate; keep warm.

2. Add sausage to skillet; cook 6 to 8 minutes or until no longer pink, stirring to break up meat. Remove from heat; stir in stuffing mix, water, bell peppers and poultry seasoning, if desired, until just blended.

3. Arrange pork, seasoned side up, over stuffing mixture. Cover; bake 15 minutes or until pork is no longer pink in center. Let stand 5 minutes before serving.

4 thin bone-in pork chops (1 pound)

$1/4$ teaspoon dried thyme

$1/4$ teaspoon paprika

$1/8$ teaspoon salt

$1/4$ pound 50% less fat bulk pork sausage

2 cups corn bread stuffing mix

$1^{1}/_{4}$ cups water

1 cup frozen diced green bell peppers, thawed

$1/8$ to $1/4$ teaspoon poultry seasoning (optional)

TUSCAN TURKEY AND WHITE BEAN SKILLET

MAKES 6 SERVINGS

1. Combine $1/2$ teaspoon rosemary, garlic salt and $1/4$ teaspoon pepper in small bowl; mix well. Sprinkle over turkey.

2. Heat 1 teaspoon oil in large skillet over medium heat. Add half of turkey; cook 2 to 3 minutes per side or until no longer pink in center. Remove to platter; tent with foil to keep warm. Repeat with remaining 1 teaspoon oil and turkey.

3. Add beans, tomatoes, remaining $1/2$ teaspoon rosemary and $1/4$ teaspoon pepper to skillet; bring to a boil over high heat. Reduce heat to low; simmer 5 minutes.

4. Spoon bean mixture over turkey; sprinkle with cheese.

1 teaspoon dried rosemary, divided

$1/2$ teaspoon garlic salt

$1/2$ teaspoon black pepper, divided

1 pound turkey breast cutlets, pounded to $1/4$-inch thickness

2 teaspoons canola oil

1 can (about 15 ounces) no-salt-added navy beans or Great Northern beans, rinsed and drained

1 can (about 14 ounces) fire-roasted diced tomatoes

$1/4$ cup grated Parmesan cheese

MEXICAN SKILLET TAMALE CASSEROLE

MAKES 4 SERVINGS

1. Preheat oven to 400°F. Brown beef in large ovenproof skillet over medium-high heat 6 to 8 minutes, stirring to break up meat. Drain fat. Return browned meat to skillet. Stir in corn, chiles, tomato sauce, water, taco seasoning mix and cumin; remove from heat. Smooth mixture with spoon.

2. Combine baking mix, milk and eggs in small bowl; stir until well blended. Pour evenly over meat mixture. Bake 40 minutes or until crust is golden and knife inserted into center comes out clean.

3. Sprinkle evenly with cheese. Let stand 5 minutes to allow cheese to melt and flavors to blend. Top as desired.

1 pound ground beef

1 cup frozen corn, thawed

1 can (4 ounces) diced green chiles

1 can (8 ounces) tomato sauce

$1/2$ cup water

1 package (about 1 ounce) taco seasoning mix

$1/2$ teaspoon ground cumin

$1/2$ cup biscuit baking mix

1 cup whole milk

2 eggs

6 ounces shredded Monterey Jack cheese or Mexican four-cheese blend (about $1 1/2$ cups)

Optional toppings: sour cream, sliced olives, chopped fresh tomatoes and chopped fresh cilantro

CLASSIC LASAGNA

MAKES 6 TO 8 SERVINGS

1. Preheat oven to 350°F. Spray 13×9-inch deep baking dish with nonstick cooking spray.

2. Heat oil in large saucepan over medium-high heat. Add beef; cook and stir 10 minutes or until meat is no longer pink, breaking up meat with wooden spoon; drain fat. Add pasta sauce; bring to a boil. Reduce heat to medium-low; cook 15 minutes, stirring occasionally.

3. Meanwhile, beat egg in medium bowl. Stir in ricotta, 1/2 cup Parmesan cheese, parsley, garlic, salt and pepper until blended.

4. Spread 1/4 cup beef mixture in prepared baking dish. Top with 3 noodles, breaking to fit if necessary. Spread one third of ricotta mixture over noodles. Sprinkle with 1 cup mozzarella cheese; top with 2 cups beef mixture. Repeat layers of noodles, ricotta mixture, mozzarella cheese and beef mixture two times. Top with remaining 3 noodles, beef mixture, 1 cup mozzarella cheese and 1/4 cup Parmesan cheese. Cover dish with foil sprayed with cooking spray.

5. Bake 30 minutes. Remove foil; bake 10 to 15 minutes or until hot and bubbly. Let stand 10 minutes before serving.

1 tablespoon olive oil

1 pound ground beef

2 jars (24 ounces each) tomato, basil and garlic pasta sauce

1 egg

1 container (15 ounces) ricotta cheese

3/4 cup grated Parmesan cheese, divided

1/2 cup minced fresh parsley

1 clove garlic, minced

1/2 teaspoon salt

1/4 teaspoon black pepper

12 uncooked no-boil lasagna noodles

4 cups (16 ounces) shredded mozzarella cheese

CHICKEN SKILLET SUPPER

MAKES 4 TO 6 SERVINGS

1. Mix salt, pepper, paprika and garlic powder in small bowl; rub over chicken. Heat oil in large skillet over medium heat; add chicken, skin-side down. Cover; cook 10 minutes. Add water; cover and cook 30 minutes, turning chicken every 10 minutes. Remove chicken to plate.

2. Add onion, potato and almonds, if desired, to pan juices; cook about 3 minutes or until onion is tender. Add tomato sauce, broth and sugar; cook until liquid comes to a boil. Add beans and chicken; cover and cook 10 minutes or until beans are tender. Serve hot.

1 teaspoon salt

1/4 teaspoon black pepper

1/4 teaspoon paprika

1/8 teaspoon garlic powder

1 cut-up whole chicken (about 3 pounds)

1 tablespoon vegetable oil

2 tablespoons water

1 medium onion, chopped

1 medium potato, peeled and cut into 2×1/4-inch pieces

1 tablespoon slivered almonds (optional)

1 can (8 ounces) tomato sauce

1 cup chicken broth

1 teaspoon sugar

1 package (10 ounces) frozen mixed vegetables or French-cut green beans

CHICKEN AND HERB STEW

MAKES 4 SERVINGS

1. Combine flour, salt, black pepper and paprika in shallow dish; stir until well blended. Coat chicken with flour mixture; shake off excess.

2. Heat oil in large skillet over medium-high heat. Add chicken; cook 10 minutes or until browned on both sides, turning once. Remove to plate.

3. Add potatoes, carrots, bell pepper, onion and garlic to same skillet; cook and stir 6 minutes or until vegetables are lightly browned. Add water, wine and bouillon; cook 1 minute, scraping up any browned bits from bottom of skillet. Stir in oregano and rosemary.

4. Place chicken on top of vegetable mixture, turning several times to coat. Cover and simmer 45 to 50 minutes or until chicken is cooked through (165°F), turning occasionally. Garnish with parsley.

$\frac{1}{2}$ cup all-purpose flour

$\frac{1}{2}$ teaspoon salt

$\frac{1}{4}$ teaspoon black pepper

$\frac{1}{4}$ teaspoon paprika

4 chicken drumsticks

4 chicken thighs

2 tablespoons olive oil

12 ounces unpeeled new red potatoes, quartered

2 carrots, quartered lengthwise, then cut crosswise into 3-inch pieces

1 green bell pepper, cut into thin strips

$\frac{3}{4}$ cup chopped onion

2 cloves garlic, minced

1$\frac{3}{4}$ cups water

$\frac{1}{4}$ cup dry white wine

2 cubes chicken bouillon

1 tablespoon chopped fresh oregano

1 teaspoon chopped fresh rosemary leaves

2 tablespoons chopped fresh Italian parsley (optional)

CHICKEN SCARPIELLO

MAKES 4 TO 6 SERVINGS

1. Heat 1 tablespoon oil in large skillet over medium-high heat. Add sausage; cook about 10 minutes or until well browned on all sides, stirring occasionally. Remove sausage from skillet; set aside.

2. Heat 1 tablespoon oil in same skillet. Sprinkle chicken with $1/2$ teaspoon salt; arrange skin side down in single layer in skillet (cook in batches if necessary). Cook about 6 minutes per side or until browned. Remove chicken from skillet; set aside. Drain oil from skillet.

3. Heat remaining 1 tablespoon oil in skillet. Add onion and $1/2$ teaspoon salt; cook and stir 2 minutes or until onion is softened, scraping up any browned bits from bottom of skillet. Add bell peppers and garlic; cook and stir 5 minutes. Stir in wine; cook until liquid is reduced by half. Stir in broth, cherry peppers, cherry pepper liquid and oregano. Season with additional salt and black pepper; bring to a simmer.

4. Return sausage and chicken along with any accumulated juices to skillet. Partially cover skillet; simmer 10 minutes. Uncover; simmer 15 minutes or until chicken is cooked through (165°F). Sprinkle with parsley.

TIP: If too much liquid remains in the skillet when the chicken is cooked through, remove the chicken and sausage and continue simmering the sauce to reduce it slightly.

3 tablespoons extra virgin olive oil, divided

1 pound spicy Italian sausage, cut into 1-inch pieces

1 cut-up whole chicken (about 3 pounds)*

1 teaspoon salt, divided

1 large onion, chopped

2 red, yellow or orange bell peppers, cut into $1/4$-inch strips

3 cloves garlic, minced

$1/2$ cup dry white wine

$1/2$ cup chicken broth

$1/2$ cup coarsely chopped seeded hot cherry peppers

$1/2$ cup liquid from cherry pepper jar

1 teaspoon dried oregano

Additional salt and black pepper

$1/4$ cup chopped fresh Italian parsley

Or purchase 2 bone-in chicken leg quarters and 2 chicken breasts; separate drumsticks and thighs and cut breasts in half.

EASY CHICKEN CHALUPAS

MAKES 6 SERVINGS

1. Preheat oven to 350°F. Lightly spray 13×9-inch baking dish with nonstick cooking spray. Shred chicken; discard skin and bones.

2. Place 2 tortillas in prepared baking dish, overlapping slightly. Layer tortillas with 1 cup chicken, 1/2 cup cheese and 1/4 cup of each salsa. Repeat layers three times.

3. Bake 25 minutes or until bubbly and heated through.

TIP: Serve this easy main dish with toppings such as sour cream, chopped fresh cilantro, sliced black olives, sliced green onions and sliced avocado.

1 rotisserie chicken (about 2 pounds)

8 (8-inch) flour tortillas

2 cups (8 ounces) shredded Cheddar cheese

1 cup mild green salsa

1 cup mild red salsa

30-MINUTE THURSDAY

BBQ CHICKEN FLATBREAD

MAKES 4 SERVINGS

1. Preheat oven to 400°F; place oven rack in lower third of oven. Line baking sheet with parchment paper.

2. For pickled onion, combine vinegar and sugar in small bowl; stir until sugar is dissolved. Add red onion; cover and let stand at room temperature while preparing flatbread. Combine chicken and barbecue sauce in medium bowl; toss to coat.

3. Roll out dough into 11×9-inch rectangle on lightly floured surface. Transfer dough to prepared baking sheet; top with cheese and barbecue chicken mixture.

4. Bake about 12 minutes or until crust is golden brown and crisp and cheese is melted. Drain liquid from red onion; sprinkle over flatbread. Garnish with green onion and cilantro. Serve immediately.

3 tablespoons red wine vinegar

2 teaspoons sugar

$1/4$ red onion, thinly sliced (about $1/3$ cup)

3 cups shredded rotisserie chicken

$1/2$ cup barbecue sauce

1 package (about 14 ounces) refrigerated pizza dough

All-purpose flour, for dusting

$1 1/2$ cups (6 ounces) shredded mozzarella cheese

1 green onion, thinly sliced on bias

2 tablespoons chopped fresh cilantro

QUICK PASTA PUTTANESCA

MAKES 6 TO 8 SERVINGS

1. Cook spaghetti according to package directions; drain and return to saucepan. Add 1 teaspoon oil; toss to coat. Cover and keep warm.

2. Heat remaining 3 tablespoons oil in large skillet over medium-high heat. Add red pepper flakes; cook and stir until sizzling. Add onion and garlic; cook and stir 1 minute. Add tuna; cook and stir 2 to 3 minutes. Add tomatoes, tomato sauce, olives and capers; cook until sauce is heated through, stirring frequently.

3. Add sauce to pasta; stir until coated. Serve immediately.

1 package (16 ounces) uncooked spaghetti or linguine

3 tablespoons plus 1 teaspoon olive oil, divided

1/4 to 1 teaspoon red pepper flakes*

1 tablespoon dried minced onion

1 teaspoon minced garlic

2 cans (6 ounces each) chunk light tuna packed in water, drained

1 can (28 ounces) diced tomatoes

1 can (8 ounces) tomato sauce

24 pitted kalamata or black olives

2 tablespoons capers, drained

For a mildly spicy dish, use 1/4 teaspoon red pepper flakes. For a very spicy dish, use 1 teaspoon red pepper flakes.

FABULOUS FETA FRITTATA

MAKES 4 SERVINGS

1. Preheat broiler.

2. Beat eggs, basil, cream, salt and pepper in medium bowl. Melt butter in large ovenproof skillet over medium heat, tilting skillet to coat bottom and side.

3. Pour egg mixture into skillet. Cover and cook 8 to 10 minutes or until eggs are set around edge (center will be wet).

4. Sprinkle cheese and pine nuts evenly over top. Transfer to broiler; broil 4 to 5 inches from heat source 2 minutes or until center is set and pine nuts are golden brown. Cut into wedges to serve.

TIP: If skillet is not ovenproof, wrap the handle in heavy-duty foil.

- 8 eggs
- $1/4$ cup chopped fresh basil
- $1/4$ cup whipping cream or half-and-half
- $1/4$ teaspoon salt
- $1/4$ teaspoon freshly ground black pepper
- 2 tablespoons butter or olive oil
- 1 package (4 ounces) crumbled feta cheese with basil, olives and sun-dried tomatoes *or* 1 cup crumbled feta cheese
- $1/4$ cup pine nuts

SALMON AND CRAB CAKES

MAKES 4 SERVINGS

1. Flake salmon and crabmeat into medium bowl. Add egg, mayonnaise, parsley, dill weed, salt, pepper, mustard and Worcestershire sauce; stir until well blended.

2. Place bread crumbs in shallow dish. Drop heaping $1/3$ cup salmon mixture into bread crumbs; shape into thick patty. Repeat with remaining mixture.

3. Spray large nonstick skillet with nonstick cooking spray. Cook salmon and crab cakes, covered, over medium heat 5 to 8 minutes, turning once.

$1/2$ **pound cooked salmon**

$1/2$ **pound cooked crabmeat***

1 **egg, lightly beaten** or $1/4$ **cup cholesterol-free egg substitute**

$11/2$ **tablespoons mayonnaise**

1 **tablespoon minced fresh parsley**

1 **teaspoon dried dill weed**

$1/2$ **teaspoon salt**

$1/2$ **teaspoon black pepper**

$1/2$ **teaspoon mustard**

$1/4$ **teaspoon Worcestershire sauce**

$1/4$ **cup plain dry bread crumbs**

Lump crabmeat works best.

SOUTHWESTERN CHICKEN AND BLACK BEAN SKILLET

MAKES 4 SERVINGS

1. Combine cumin, chili powder and salt in small bowl; sprinkle evenly over both sides of chicken.

2. Heat oil in large nonstick skillet over medium-high heat. Add chicken; cook 4 minutes, turning once. Remove to plate.

3. Add onion to same skillet; cook and stir 1 minute. Add bell pepper; cook 5 minutes, stirring occasionally. Stir in beans and salsa.

4. Place chicken on top of bean mixture. Cover and cook 6 to 7 minutes or until chicken is no longer pink in center. Garnish with cilantro.

1 teaspoon ground cumin

1 teaspoon chili powder

$1/2$ teaspoon salt

4 boneless skinless chicken breasts (about 1 pound)

2 teaspoons canola or vegetable oil

1 cup chopped onion

1 red bell pepper, chopped

1 can (about 15 ounces) black beans, rinsed and drained

$1/2$ cup chunky salsa

$1/4$ cup chopped fresh cilantro or thinly sliced green onions (optional)

CHICKEN, HUMMUS AND VEGETABLE WRAPS
MAKES 4 SERVINGS

Spread hummus evenly over wraps all the way to edges. Arrange chicken over hummus; sprinkle with hot pepper sauce, if desired. Top with carrots, cucumber, radishes and mint. Roll up tightly. Cut in half diagonally.

VARIATION: Substitute alfalfa sprouts for the radishes.

$3/4$ cup hummus (regular, roasted red pepper or roasted garlic)

4 (8- to 10-inch) sun-dried tomato *or* spinach wraps *or* whole wheat tortillas

2 cups chopped cooked chicken breast

Chipotle hot pepper sauce or Louisiana-style hot pepper sauce (optional)

$1/2$ cup shredded carrots

$1/2$ cup chopped unpeeled cucumber

$1/2$ cup thinly sliced radishes

2 tablespoons chopped fresh mint or basil

ORANGE CHICKEN STIR-FRY OVER QUINOA

MAKES 4 SERVINGS

1. Place quinoa in fine-mesh strainer; rinse well under cold running water. Bring 1 cup water to a boil in medium saucepan; stir in quinoa. Reduce heat to low; cover and simmer 10 to 15 minutes or until quinoa is tender and water is absorbed.

2. Meanwhile, heat 1 teaspoon oil in large skillet over medium-high heat. Add chicken; cook and stir 4 to 6 minutes or until no longer pink. Remove to plate; keep warm.

3. Stir orange juice and soy sauce into cornstarch in small bowl until smooth; set aside. Heat remaining 1 teaspoon oil in skillet. Add green onions and ginger; stir-fry 1 to 2 minutes. Add snow peas and carrots; stir-fry 4 to 5 minutes or until carrots are crisp-tender.

4. Return chicken to skillet. Stir orange juice mixture; add to skillet. Bring to a boil. Reduce heat; simmer until slightly thickened.

5. Serve chicken and vegetables over quinoa; sprinkle with red pepper flakes, if desired.

- 1/2 cup uncooked quinoa
- 1 cup water
- 2 teaspoons vegetable oil, divided
- 1 pound boneless skinless chicken breasts, cut into thin strips
- 1 cup fresh squeezed orange juice (2 to 3 oranges)
- 1 tablespoon reduced-sodium soy sauce
- 1 tablespoon cornstarch
- 1/2 cup sliced green onions
- 2 tablespoons grated fresh ginger
- 6 ounces snow peas, ends trimmed
- 1 cup thinly sliced carrots
- 1/4 teaspoon red pepper flakes (optional)

BROILED SALMON WITH CUCUMBER YOGURT

MAKES 4 SERVINGS

1. Combine yogurt and cucumber in medium bowl; cover and refrigerate.

2. Preheat broiler. Place salmon, skin side down, on foil-lined baking sheet. Stir honey, mustard and curry powder in small bowl until smooth. Spread on salmon. Broil about 5 inches from heat 10 minutes or until opaque in center. Serve with cucumber yogurt.

SERVING SUGGESTION: Serve with brown rice pilaf and asparagus.

- 1 cup plain nonfat yogurt
- 2/3 cup finely chopped cucumber
- 1 pound salmon fillet, cut into 4 pieces
- 2 teaspoons honey
- 1 teaspoon Dijon mustard
- 1/4 teaspoon curry powder

STIR-FRY VEGETABLE PITA PIZZAS

MAKES 4 SERVINGS

1. Preheat broiler. Heat oil in large nonstick skillet over medium-high heat. Add bell pepper; stir-fry 1 minute. Add mushrooms, zucchini and garlic; stir-fry 4 minutes or until vegetables are crisp-tender. Stir in black pepper; remove from heat.

2. Use small knife to cut around edges of pita rounds and split each into 2 rounds. Place pita rounds on baking sheet. Broil 4 to 5 inches from heat source 1 minute or until lightly toasted. Turn pitas; top with pizza sauce, vegetables and cheese. Return to broiler; broil 3 minutes or until cheese is melted. Top with basil.

TIP: Choose zucchini that are heavy for their size, firm and well shaped. They should have a bright color and be free of cuts and any soft spots. Small zucchini are more tender because they were harvested when young. They should be rinsed well before using, but peeling is not necessary.

1 teaspoon olive oil

1 red bell pepper, sliced

1½ cups (4 ounces) baby portobello mushrooms, thinly sliced

1 medium zucchini, thinly sliced

2 cloves garlic, minced

¼ teaspoon black pepper

2 (6-inch) whole wheat pita bread rounds

¼ cup pizza sauce

½ cup (2 ounces) shredded or grated Parmesan cheese

¼ cup chopped fresh basil

QUICK TUSCAN BEAN, TOMATO AND SPINACH SOUP

MAKES 4 SERVINGS

1. Combine tomatoes, broth, sugar, basil and Worcestershire sauce in Dutch oven or large saucepan; bring to a boil over high heat. Reduce heat to low. Simmer, uncovered, 10 minutes.

2. Stir in beans and spinach; cook 5 minutes or until spinach is tender.

3. Remove from heat; stir in oil just before serving.

2 cans (about 14 ounces each) diced tomatoes with onions

1 can (about 14 ounces) chicken broth

2 teaspoons sugar

2 teaspoons dried basil

$3/4$ teaspoon reduced-sodium Worcestershire sauce

1 can (about 15 ounces) small white beans, rinsed and drained

3 ounces fresh baby spinach leaves or chopped spinach leaves, stems removed

2 teaspoons extra virgin olive oil

BRATWURST SKILLET
MAKES 4 SERVINGS

1. Heat large skillet over medium heat. Add bratwurst; cover and cook about 5 minutes or until browned and no longer pink in center. Transfer bratwurst to plate. Cover and keep warm.

2. Drain all but 1 tablespoon drippings from skillet. Add onions, bell peppers, paprika and caraway seeds. Cook and stir about 5 minutes or until vegetables are tender.

3. Combine bratwurst and vegetables. Serve immediately.

TIP: To make this even speedier, purchase a packaged stir-fry pepper and onion mix and use in place of the bell peppers and onions.

1 **pound bratwurst links, cut into $1/2$-inch slices**

$1^1/_2$ **cups sliced onions**

$1^1/_2$ **cups green bell pepper strips**

$1^1/_2$ **cups red bell pepper strips**

1 **teaspoon paprika**

1 **teaspoon caraway seeds**

CHICKEN AND VEGGIE FAJITAS

MAKES 6 SERVINGS

1. Toss chicken with oregano, chili powder and garlic salt in large bowl. Heat large skillet coated with nonstick cooking spray over medium-high heat. Add chicken; cook and stir 5 to 6 minutes or until cooked through. Remove to bowl; set aside.

2. Add bell peppers and onion to same skillet; cook and stir 2 minutes over medium heat. Add salsa; cover and cook 6 to 8 minutes or until vegetables are tender. Uncover; stir in chicken and any juices from bowl. Cook and stir 2 minutes or until heated through.

3. Serve mixture on top of tortillas topped with cilantro and sour cream, if desired.

1 **pound boneless skinless chicken thighs, cut crosswise into strips**

1 **teaspoon dried oregano**

1 **teaspoon chili powder**

1/2 **teaspoon garlic salt**

2 **bell peppers (preferably 1 red and 1 green), cut into thin strips**

4 **thin slices large sweet or yellow onion, separated into rings**

1/2 **cup salsa**

6 **(6-inch) flour tortillas, warmed**

1/2 **cup chopped fresh cilantro or green onions**

Sour cream (optional)

FAMILY FAVORITES FRIDAY

MOM'S BAKED MOSTACCIOLI

MAKES 8 SERVINGS

1. Preheat oven to 350°F. Spray 13×9-inch casserole with nonstick cooking spray.

2. Combine ricotta cheese, egg substitute and Parmesan cheese in medium bowl. Season with garlic powder, pepper and Italian seasoning; mix well.

3. Place half of pasta and half the sauce in prepared casserole. Spread ricotta mixture evenly over pasta. Spoon remaining pasta and sauce over ricotta mixture. Top with mozzarella cheese.

4. Bake 30 minutes or until hot and bubbly.

1 container (16 ounces) part-skim ricotta cheese

$\frac{1}{2}$ cup cholesterol-free egg substitute

$\frac{1}{4}$ cup grated Parmesan cheese

Garlic powder

Black pepper

Italian seasoning

1 package (16 ounces) mostaccioli, cooked and drained

1 jar (26 ounces) prepared pasta sauce

$1\frac{1}{2}$ cups (6 ounces) shredded mozzarella cheese

ROASTED CHICKEN WITH VEGETABLES

MAKES 4 SERVINGS

1. Preheat oven to 425°F. Brush large baking sheet with oil.

2. Whisk ⅓ cup oil, vinegar, garlic, salt, onion powder, paprika and pepper in large bowl until well blended. Remove half of mixture to another large bowl; add chicken to first bowl; turn to coat.

3. Place chicken, skin side up on prepared baking sheet. Roast 30 minutes.

4. Add vegetables to other bowl with oil mixture; turn to coat. Push chicken to one side of baking sheet. Arrange vegetables on other half of baking sheet.*

5. Roast 30 to 35 minutes or until chicken is 165°F. Serve chicken with vegetables. Garnish with parsley and lemon slices.

*If your baking sheet is not large enough for the chicken and vegetables, use 2 baking sheets.

⅓ cup olive oil, plus additional for pan

2 tablespoons red wine vinegar

2 cloves garlic, minced

1 teaspoon salt

1 teaspoon onion powder

¼ teaspoon paprika

¼ teaspoon black pepper

8 bone-in, skin-on chicken thighs, wings and legs (about 3 pounds)

3 cups chopped vegetables, like carrots, red onion, eggplant, zucchini and yellow squash

Chopped fresh parsley and lemon slices (optional)

SPAGHETTI & MEATBALLS

MAKES 4 SERVINGS

1. Preheat oven to 450°F. Spray baking sheet with nonstick cooking spray. Cook spaghetti according to package directions, omitting salt and fat. Drain and keep warm.

2. Combine beef, sausage, egg white, bread crumbs and oregano in medium bowl; mix well. Shape mixture into 16 (1½-inch) meatballs. Place on prepared baking sheet; coat with cooking spray. Bake 12 minutes, turning once.

3. Pour pasta sauce into large skillet. Add meatballs; cook over medium heat 9 minutes or until sauce is heated through and meatballs are cooked through (160°F), stirring occasionally. Divide spaghetti among 4 plates. Top with meatballs and sauce; sprinkle with basil and cheese.

6 ounces uncooked multigrain or whole wheat spaghetti

¾ pound extra lean ground beef

¼ pound hot turkey Italian sausage, casing removed

1 egg white

2 tablespoons plain dry bread crumbs

1 teaspoon dried oregano

2 cups tomato-basil pasta sauce

3 tablespoons chopped fresh basil

2 tablespoons grated Parmesan cheese

TUNA NOODLE CASSEROLE

MAKES 4 SERVINGS

1. Preheat oven to 375°F. Spray 8-inch square baking dish with nonstick cooking spray.

2. Cook pasta according to package directions until al dente. Drain and set aside.

3. Meanwhile, melt butter in large deep skillet over medium heat. Add onion; cook and stir 3 minutes. Add celery and bell pepper; cook and stir 3 minutes. Add flour, salt and white pepper to vegetables; cook and stir 1 minute. Gradually stir in milk; bring to a boil. Cook and stir 2 minutes or until thickened. Remove from heat.

4. Add pasta, tuna and ¼ cup cheese to skillet; stir until pasta is well coated. Pour tuna mixture into prepared dish; sprinkle evenly with remaining ¼ cup cheese.

5. Bake, uncovered, 20 to 25 minutes or until hot and bubbly.

7 ounces (2 cups) uncooked elbow macaroni

2 tablespoons butter

¾ cup chopped onion (½ large onion)

½ cup thinly sliced celery (2 stalks)

½ cup finely chopped red bell pepper

2 tablespoons all-purpose flour

½ teaspoon salt

⅛ teaspoon white pepper

1½ cups milk

1 can (6 ounces) albacore tuna in water, drained

½ cup grated Parmesan cheese, divided

SUPER MEATBALL SLIDERS

MAKES 24 SLIDERS

1. Preheat oven to 350°F. Combine cranberry sauce, tomato sauce and red pepper flakes, if desired, in medium bowl.

2. Combine ground beef, bread crumbs, egg and soup mix in large bowl; mix well. Shape mixture into 24 meatballs (about $1\frac{3}{4}$ inches). Place in 13×9-inch baking pan or glass baking dish; pour sauce over meatballs, making sure all meatballs are covered in sauce.

3. Bake 40 to 45 minutes or until meatballs are cooked through (160°F), basting with sauce once or twice during cooking.

4. Place arugula leaves on rolls, if desired; top with meatballs and cheese. Spoon sauce from pan over meatballs.

1 can (15 ounces) whole berry cranberry sauce

1 can (about 15 ounces) tomato sauce

$\frac{1}{8}$ teaspoon red pepper flakes (optional)

2 pounds ground beef or turkey

$\frac{3}{4}$ cup plain bread crumbs

1 egg, lightly beaten

1 package (1 ounce) dry onion soup mix

Baby arugula leaves (optional)

24 small potato rolls or dinner rolls, split

6 slices (1 ounce each) provolone cheese, cut into quarters

TUSCAN BAKED RIGATONI
MAKES 6 TO 8 SERVINGS

1. Preheat oven to 350°F. Coat 4-quart casserole with nonstick cooking spray; set aside.

2. Brown sausage in large skillet over medium-high heat, stirring to break up meat; drain fat. Transfer sausage to large bowl. Add rigatoni and fontina cheese; mix well.

3. Heat oil in same skillet; add fennel and garlic. Cook and stir over medium heat 3 minutes or until fennel is tender. Add tomatoes, cream, salt and pepper; cook and stir until slightly thickened. Stir in spinach, beans and pine nuts; cook until heated through.

4. Pour sauce mixture over pasta mixture; toss to coat. Transfer to prepared casserole; sprinkle evenly with Parmesan cheese. Bake 30 minutes or until bubbly and heated through.

1 pound bulk Italian sausage

1 package (16 ounces) rigatoni pasta, cooked, drained and kept warm

2 cups (8 ounces) shredded fontina cheese

2 tablespoons olive oil

2 bulbs fennel, thinly sliced

4 cloves garlic, minced

1 can (28 ounces) crushed tomatoes

1 cup whipping cream

1 teaspoon salt

1 teaspoon black pepper

8 cups packed fresh spinach

1 can (about 15 ounces) cannellini beans, rinsed and drained

2 tablespoons pine nuts

1/2 cup grated Parmesan cheese

SKILLET LASAGNA WITH VEGETABLES

MAKES 6 SERVINGS

1. Heat large skillet over medium-high heat. Add sausage, ground turkey, celery and onion; cook and stir 6 to 8 minutes or until turkey is no longer pink. Stir in marinara sauce and water; bring to a boil. Stir in pasta. Reduce heat to medium-low; cover and simmer 12 minutes.

2. Stir in zucchini and bell pepper; cover and simmer 2 minutes. Uncover and simmer 4 to 6 minutes or until vegetables are crisp-tender.

3. Sprinkle with mozzarella cheese. Combine ricotta and Parmesan cheese in small bowl; stir to blend. Drop by rounded teaspoonfuls on top of mixture in skillet. Remove from heat; cover and let stand 10 minutes.

- $1/2$ pound hot Italian turkey sausage, casings removed
- $1/2$ pound ground turkey
- 2 stalks celery, sliced
- $1/3$ cup chopped onion
- 2 cups marinara sauce
- $1 1/3$ cups water
- 4 ounces uncooked bowtie (farfalle) pasta
- 1 medium zucchini, halved lengthwise, then cut crosswise into $1/2$-inch slices (2 cups)
- $3/4$ cup chopped green or yellow bell pepper
- $1/2$ cup (2 ounces) shredded part-skim mozzarella cheese
- $1/2$ cup reduced-fat ricotta cheese
- 2 tablespoons finely grated Parmesan cheese

SESAME CHICKEN

MAKES 4 SERVINGS

1. Combine chicken and ⅓ cup teriyaki sauce in medium bowl; toss to coat. Marinate in refrigerator 15 to 20 minutes.

2. Drain chicken; discard marinade. Stir remaining ⅓ cup teriyaki sauce into cornstarch in small bowl until smooth.

3. Heat peanut oil in wok or large skillet over medium-high heat. Add chicken and garlic; stir-fry 3 minutes or until chicken is cooked through. Stir cornstarch mixture; add to wok. Cook and stir 1 minute or until sauce boils and thickens. Stir in green onions, sesame seeds and sesame oil.

1 pound boneless skinless chicken breasts or thighs, cut into 1-inch pieces

⅔ cup teriyaki sauce, divided

2 teaspoons cornstarch

1 tablespoon peanut or vegetable oil

2 cloves garlic, minced

2 green onions, cut into ½-inch slices

1 tablespoon sesame seeds, toasted*

1 teaspoon dark sesame oil

To toast sesame seeds, spread seeds in small skillet. Shake skillet over medium-low heat 3 minutes or until seeds begin to pop and turn golden.

CHICKEN FAJITA NACHOS
MAKES 4 SERVINGS

1. Heat 1 tablespoon oil in large skillet over medium-high heat. Add bell peppers and onion; cook 5 minutes or until tender and browned in spots, stirring frequently. Transfer to large bowl; stir in 1 tablespoon fajita seasoning mix and 1 tablespoon water.

2. Heat remaining 1 tablespoon oil in same skillet over medium-high heat. Add chicken; cook 7 to 10 minutes or until cooked through, stirring occasionally. Add remaining 1 tablespoon fajita seasoning mix and 1 tablespoon water; cook and stir until chicken is coated.

3. Preheat broiler. Place chips in 11×7-inch baking dish or pan; top with vegetables, chicken, Cheddar and Monterey Jack cheeses and jalapeño pepper.

4. Broil 2 to 4 minutes or until cheeses are melted. Top with lettuce, 1/2 cup salsa, sour cream and guacamole, if desired. Serve immediately with additional salsa.

2 tablespoons vegetable oil, divided

2 red bell peppers, cut into thin strips

1 large onion, halved and thinly sliced

2 tablespoons fajita seasoning mix (from 1 1/4-ounce package), divided

2 tablespoons water, divided

1 large boneless skinless chicken breast (about 12 ounces), cut into 2×1-inch strips

4 cups tortilla chips (about 30 chips)

1/2 cup (2 ounces) shredded Cheddar cheese

1/2 cup (2 ounces) shredded Monterey Jack cheese

1 jalapeño pepper,* seeded and thinly sliced

1 cup shredded lettuce

1/2 cup salsa, plus additional for serving

Sour cream and guacamole (optional)

*Jalapeño peppers can sting and irritate the skin, so wear rubber gloves when handling peppers and do not touch your eyes.

GUACAMOLE BURGERS

MAKES 4 SERVINGS

1. Mash avocado in medium bowl. Stir in tomato, cilantro, 1 teaspoon lime juice, minced jalapeño pepper and $1/8$ teaspoon salt; mix well. Cover and refrigerate until ready to use. Combine sour cream, mayonnaise, remaining 1 teaspoon lime juice and cumin in small bowl; mix well. Cover and refrigerate until ready to use.

2. Heat 2 teaspoons oil in large skillet over medium-high heat. Add onion; cook about 8 minutes or until onion is very tender and begins to turn golden, stirring occasionally. (Add a few teaspoons water to skillet if onion begins to burn.) Remove to bowl. Add remaining 2 teaspoons oil to skillet. Add bell peppers; cook and stir 5 minutes or until tender. Remove to bowl with onion; season vegetables with remaining $1/8$ teaspoon salt.

3. Preheat grill or broiler. Shape beef into 4 (5-inch) patties. Grill or broil patties about 5 minutes per side or until cooked through (160°F). Top patties with cheese slices during last minute of cooking.

4. Lightly toast buns. Spread sour cream mixture over bottom halves of buns. Top with vegetables, burgers, guacamole, fire-roasted jalapeño peppers and top halves of buns.

1 small avocado

2 tablespoons finely chopped fresh tomato

1 tablespoon chopped fresh cilantro

2 teaspoons lime juice, divided

1 teaspoon minced jalapeño pepper*

$1/4$ teaspoon salt, divided

2 tablespoons sour cream

2 tablespoons mayonnaise

$1/2$ teaspoon ground cumin

4 teaspoons vegetable oil, divided

1 onion, cut into thin slices

1 green bell pepper, cut into thin slices

1 red bell pepper, cut into thin slices

$1^{1}/4$ pounds ground beef

4 slices Monterey Jack cheese

4 hamburger buns

1 can (4 ounces) diced fire-roasted jalapeño peppers, drained

*Jalapeño peppers can sting and irritate the skin, so wear rubber gloves when handling peppers and do not touch your eyes.

BRUSCHETTA CHICKEN FETTUCCINE

MAKES 4 SERVINGS

1. For glaze, combine balsamic vinegar, brown sugar, molasses and ¼ teaspoon salt in small saucepan; bring to a simmer over medium heat. Cook about 10 minutes or until reduced by half. Set aside to cool.

2. For sauce, combine tomatoes, tomato sauce, ¼ cup oil, basil, white wine vinegar, garlic, ¾ teaspoon salt and ½ teaspoon pepper in medium bowl; mix well.

3. If necessary, pound chicken to ¾-inch thickness between 2 sheets of plastic wrap. Season with salt, pepper and garlic powder. Heat 1 tablespoon oil in large skillet over medium-high heat. Add chicken; cook 5 minutes per side or until golden brown and cooked through. Remove to plate; cover loosely with foil to keep warm.

4. Meanwhile, cook fettuccine in large saucepan until al dente. Drain in colander; return empty saucepan to stove. Add sauce to saucepan; cook and stir over high heat 2 minutes or until heated through. Add fettuccine and grated Parmesan to saucepan; toss to coat.

5. Slice chicken. Divide pasta among 4 serving bowls; drizzle with glaze. Top each serving with sliced chicken breast; garnish with shaved Parmesan and parsley. Serve immediately.

BALSAMIC GLAZE

- ¼ cup balsamic vinegar
- 2 tablespoons packed brown sugar
- 1 teaspoon molasses
- ¼ teaspoon salt

BRUSCHETTA SAUCE

- 4 cups diced plum tomatoes (about 4 medium)
- ½ cup tomato sauce
- ¼ cup olive oil
- ¼ cup chopped fresh basil
- 1 tablespoon white wine vinegar
- 2 cloves garlic, minced
- ¾ teaspoon salt
- ½ teaspoon black pepper

CHICKEN

- 4 boneless skinless chicken breasts (4 ounces each)
  Salt and black pepper
- ¼ teaspoon garlic powder
- 1 tablespoon olive oil
- 1 package (16 ounces) uncooked fettuccine
- ¼ cup grated Parmesan cheese
  Shaved Parmesan (optional)
  Chopped fresh parsley (optional)

VEGETABLE PENNE ITALIANO

MAKES 4 SERVINGS

1. Heat oil in large skillet over medium-high heat. Add bell peppers, onion and garlic; cook and stir 8 minutes or until vegetables are crisp-tender.

2. Add tomato paste, salt, sugar, Italian seasoning and black pepper; cook and stir 1 minute. Stir in tomatoes with juice. Reduce heat to medium-low; cook 15 minutes or until vegetables are tender and sauce is thickened.

3. Meanwhile, cook pasta in large saucepan of salted water according to package directions for al dente. Drain pasta; return to saucepan. Add sauce; stir gently to coat. Divide among 4 serving bowls; top with cheese and basil.

1 tablespoon olive oil

1 red bell pepper, cut into $1/2$-inch pieces

1 green bell pepper, cut into $1/2$-inch pieces

1 medium sweet onion, halved and thinly sliced

3 cloves garlic, minced

2 tablespoons tomato paste

2 teaspoons salt

1 teaspoon sugar

1 teaspoon Italian seasoning

$1/4$ teaspoon black pepper

1 can (28 ounces) Italian plum tomatoes, chopped, juice reserved

8 ounces uncooked penne pasta

Grated Parmesan cheese

Chopped fresh basil

FISH & CHIPS

MAKES 4 SERVINGS

1. Combine flour, beer and 2 teaspoons oil in small bowl. Cover and refrigerate 1 to 2 hours.

2. Pour 2 inches oil into large heavy skillet; heat to 365°F over medium heat. Add potato wedges in batches. (*Do not crowd.*) Fry 4 to 6 minutes or until browned, turning once. (Allow temperature of oil to return to 365°F between batches.) Drain on paper towels; sprinkle lightly with salt. Reserve oil to fry cod.

3. Stir egg yolk into flour mixture. Beat egg white in medium bowl with electric mixer at medium-high speed until soft peaks form. Fold egg white into flour mixture.

4. Return oil to 365°F. Dip fish pieces into batter in batches; fry 4 to 6 minutes or until batter is crispy and brown and fish begins to flake when tested with fork, turning once. (Allow temperature of oil to return to 365°F between batches.) Drain on paper towels. Serve immediately with potato wedges. Sprinkle with vinegar and serve with lemon wedges, if desired.

3/4 cup all-purpose flour

1/2 cup flat beer or lemon-lime carbonated beverage

Vegetable oil

4 medium russet potatoes, each cut into 8 wedges

Salt

1 egg, separated

1 pound cod fillets (about 6 to 8 small fillets)

Malt vinegar (optional)

Lemon wedges (optional)

CLASSIC GRILLED CHEESE

MAKES 2 SANDWICHES

1. Place 2 slices of cheese each on 2 bread slices; top with remaining bread slices. Brush outsides of sandwiches with butter.

2. Heat large skillet over medium-high heat. Cook sandwiches 3 to 5 minutes per side or until cheese melts and sandwiches are golden brown.

4 slices (about $3/4$ ounce each) American cheese

4 slices white bread

Butter, melted

SWEET TREATS FUN DAY

DOUGHNUT HOLE FONDUE

MAKES 6 SERVINGS

1. Heat cream in small saucepan until bubbles form around edge. Remove from heat. Add chocolate; let stand 2 minutes or until softened. Add butter and vanilla; whisk until smooth. Keep warm in fondue pot or transfer to serving bowl.

2. Serve with doughnut holes and fruit.

- $3/4$ cup whipping cream
- 1 cup bittersweet or semisweet chocolate chips
- 1 tablespoon butter
- $1/2$ teaspoon vanilla
- 12 to 16 doughnut holes

  Sliced fresh fruit, such as bananas, strawberries and oranges

BLACK FOREST CAKE

MAKES 12 SERVINGS

1. Preheat oven to 350°F. Grease and flour 2 (9-inch) round cake pans. Prepare cake mix according to package directions. Divide batter between prepared pans.

2. Bake 30 to 35 minutes or until toothpick inserted into centers comes out clean. Cool in pans on wire racks 10 minutes. Remove to racks; cool completely.

3. Meanwhile, drain cherries, reserving ½ cup juice. Combine reserved juice, cherries, sugar and cornstarch in medium saucepan. Cook over low heat until thickened, stirring constantly. Stir in vanilla. Prepare Frosting.

4. Split each cake layer in half horizontally with long serrated knife. Crumble one layer; set aside.

5. Reserve 1½ cups Frosting; set aside. Place one cake layer on cake plate. Spread with 1 cup Frosting; top with ¾ cup cherry topping. Top with second cake layer; repeat layers of Frosting and cherry topping. Top with third cake layer.

6. Frost side of cake with remaining Frosting. Pat reserved crumbs onto side of cake. Spoon reserved frosting into piping bag fitted with star tip. Pipe Frosting around edge of cake. Spoon remaining cherry topping onto top of cake.

FROSTING: Combine 3 cups cold whipping cream and ⅓ cup powdered sugar in chilled medium deep bowl. Beat with electric mixer at high speed until stiff peaks form.

1 package (about 18 ounces) chocolate cake mix, plus ingredients to prepare mix

2 cans (20 ounces each) tart pitted cherries, undrained

1 cup sugar

¼ cup cornstarch

1½ teaspoons vanilla

Frosting (recipe follows)

CHOCOLATE STORM
MAKES 9 SERVINGS

1. Preheat oven to 325°F. Spray 9-inch square baking pan with nonstick cooking spray.

2. Combine semisweet chocolate, bittersweet chocolate and butter in medium microwavable bowl. Microwave on HIGH 1 minute; stir and repeat. Microwave 30 seconds; stir until chocolate is melted and mixture is smooth.

3. Beat eggs, granulated sugar, vanilla and salt in large bowl with electric mixer at medium speed 1 minute. Beat at high speed 1 minute. Add half of chocolate mixture; beat at low speed until blended. Beat in remaining chocolate mixture until blended. Stir in pecans. Pour batter into prepared pan, spreading to make top of cake level and smooth.

4. Bake about 45 minutes or until center of brownie begins to firm. Cool in pan on wire rack.*

5. When ready to serve, beat cream and powdered sugar in medium bowl with electric mixer at medium-high speed until stiff peaks form. Cut cake into 9 squares. If desired, heat individual squares in microwave on HIGH 30 seconds. Top each piece with scoop of ice cream; drizzle with hot fudge. Top with whipped cream and chocolate curls, if desired.

Cake can be served soon after baking but will be more difficult to cut.

- 12 ounces semisweet chocolate, chopped
- 12 ounces bittersweet chocolate, chopped
- ³/₄ cup (1½ sticks) butter
- 5 eggs
- ²/₃ cup granulated sugar
- 2 teaspoons vanilla
- ½ teaspoon salt
- 1¼ cups chopped pecans
- 2 cups cold whipping cream
- ¼ cup powdered sugar
- 3 pints vanilla ice cream
- 1½ cups hot fudge topping, heated
- Chocolate curls (optional)

CHOCOLATE CHUNK PIZZA COOKIE

MAKES 3 PIZZA COOKIES

1. Preheat oven to 400°F. Spray 3 (6-inch) cast iron skillets, cake pans or deep-dish pizza pans with nonstick cooking spray.*

2. Combine flour, baking soda and salt in medium bowl; mix well. Beat butter, brown sugar and granulated sugar in large bowl with electric mixer at medium speed until creamy. Beat in eggs and vanilla until well blended. Gradually beat in flour mixture at low speed just until blended. Stir in chocolate chunks. Spread dough evenly in prepared pans.

3. Bake about 15 minutes or until top and edges are deep golden brown but center is still slightly soft. Top with ice cream. Serve warm.

If you don't have 3 skillets or pans, you can bake 1 cookie at a time. Refrigerate the dough between batches and make sure the skillet is completely cool before adding more dough. (Clean and spray the skillet again before adding each new batch.)

2 cups all-purpose flour

1 teaspoon baking soda

1 teaspoon salt

3/4 cup (1 1/2 sticks) butter, softened

1 cup packed brown sugar

1/4 cup granulated sugar

2 eggs

1 teaspoon vanilla

1 package (about 11 ounces) chocolate chunks

Vanilla ice cream

CHOCOLATE CHIP COOKIES

MAKES ABOUT 16 COOKIES

1. Whisk flour, baking soda and $1/2$ teaspoon salt in medium bowl.

2. Beat butter and sugars in large bowl with electric mixer at medium-high speed until light and fluffy. Add egg and vanilla; beat until blended. Add flour mixture; beat on low speed until blended. Stir in chocolate. If desired, cover dough and refrigerate up to 2 days.

3. Preheat oven to 350°F. Line baking sheets with parchment paper. For each cookie, shape about 2 tablespoons of dough into a ball; place on prepared baking sheets. Sprinkle with sea salt, if desired.

4. Bake about 12 minutes or until edges are lightly browned. Cool cookies on baking sheets 5 minutes. Remove to wire racks; cool completely.

- 2 cups all-purpose flour
- 1 teaspoon baking soda
- $1/2$ teaspoon salt
- $3/4$ cup ($1\frac{1}{2}$ sticks) butter, softened
- $3/4$ cup packed brown sugar
- $1/2$ cup granulated sugar
- 1 egg
- $1\frac{1}{4}$ teaspoons vanilla
- 8 ounces semisweet chocolate, chopped, or chocolate chips
- Flaky sea salt (optional)

TIRAMISU

MAKES 9 SERVINGS

1. Fill medium saucepan half full with water; bring to a boil over high heat. Reduce heat to low to maintain a simmer. Whisk sugar, egg yolks and 2 tablespoons cream in medium metal bowl until well blended. Place bowl over simmering water; cook 6 to 8 minutes or until thickened, whisking constantly. Remove from heat; cool slightly. Whisk in mascarpone and vanilla until smooth and well blended.

2. Pour remaining 1 cup cream into large bowl of electric stand mixer; beat at high speed until stiff peaks form. Gently fold whipped cream into mascarpone mixture until no streaks of white remain.

3. Combine coffee and liqueur in shallow bowl; mix well. Working with one at a time, dip ladyfingers briefly in coffee mixture; arrange in single layer in 9-inch square baking pan, trimming cookies to fit as necessary. Spread thin layer of custard over ladyfingers, covering completely. Dip remaining ladyfingers in remaining coffee mixture; arrange in single layer over custard. Spread remaining custard over cookies. Place cocoa in fine-mesh strainer; sprinkle over custard. Refrigerate 2 hours or overnight.

$3/4$ cup sugar

4 egg yolks

1 cup plus 2 tablespoons whipping cream, divided

16 ounces mascarpone cheese

$1/2$ teaspoon vanilla

$3/4$ cup cold strong brewed coffee

$1/4$ cup coffee-flavored liqueur

24 to 28 ladyfingers

2 teaspoons unsweetened cocoa powder

STRAWBERRY CHEESECAKE DESSERT SHOOTERS

MAKES 8 TO 10 SERVINGS

1. Place 1 cup graham cracker crumbs in medium nonstick skillet; cook and stir over medium heat about 3 minutes or until lightly browned. Transfer to small bowl; stir in butter until well blended. Press mixture evenly into 8 to 10 (3- to 4-ounce) shot glasses.

2. Combine strawberries and ¼ cup sugar in small bowl; toss to coat. Cover and refrigerate until ready to serve.

3. Beat cream cheese in medium bowl with electric mixer at medium speed until creamy. Add eggs, remaining ½ cup sugar, sour cream and vanilla; beat until well blended. Transfer to medium saucepan; cook over medium heat 5 to 6 minutes or until thickened and smooth, stirring frequently. Divide filling evenly among prepared crusts. Refrigerate 1 hour or until cold.

4. Top each serving with strawberries and whipped cream. Garnish with additional graham cracker crumbs.

TIP: For larger servings, use 4 to 5 (6- or 8-ounce) juice or stemless wine glasses. Divide crumb mixture, filling and strawberries evenly among glasses.

1 cup graham cracker crumbs, plus additional for garnish

¼ cup (½ stick) butter, melted

2 cups chopped fresh strawberries

¾ cup sugar, divided

12 ounces cream cheese, softened

2 eggs

2 tablespoons sour cream

½ teaspoon vanilla

Whipped cream

CLASSIC FLAN
MAKES 6 SERVINGS

1. Preheat oven to 300°F.

2. Combine 1 cup sugar, water and cinnamon in medium saucepan; cook over medium-high heat without stirring about 10 minutes or until sugar is melted and mixture is deep golden amber in color. Pour into 6 (6-ounce) ramekins, swirling to coat bottoms. Place ramekins in 13×9-inch baking pan.

3. Heat milk in separate medium saucepan over medium heat until bubbles begin to form around edge of pan.

4. Meanwhile, whisk eggs, egg yolks, vanilla and remaining 1/2 cup sugar in medium bowl until well blended. Whisk in 1/2 cup hot milk in thin, steady stream. Gradually whisk in remaining milk. Divide milk mixture evenly among prepared ramekins. Carefully add hot water to larger baking pan until water comes halfway up sides of ramekins. Cover ramekins with waxed paper or parchment paper.

5. Bake 1 hour 15 minutes or until custard is firm and knife inserted into custard comes out clean. Remove ramekins from baking pan; cool completely. Cover and refrigerate until cold. Run small knife around edges of ramekins; unmold flan onto serving plates.

1½ **cups sugar, divided**

1 **tablespoon water**

¼ **teaspoon ground cinnamon**

3 **cups whole milk**

3 **eggs**

3 **egg yolks**

1 **teaspoon vanilla**

RASPBERRY WHITE CHOCOLATE CHEESECAKE

MAKES 12 SERVINGS

1. Preheat oven to 350°F. Spray 9-inch springform pan with nonstick cooking spray. Line bottom and side of pan with parchment paper. Wrap outside of pan tightly with foil.

2. For crust, combine crushed cookies and butter in small bowl; mix well. Press mixture onto bottom and up side of prepared pan. Bake about 8 minutes or until firm. Remove to wire rack; cool completely. *Increase oven temperature to 450°F.*

3. Beat cream cheese in large bowl with electric mixer at low speed until creamy. Add sugar, sour cream and vanilla; beat until smooth and well blended. Add eggs, one at a time, beating until blended after each addition. Fold in chopped white chocolate with spatula. Spread one third of filling in crust. Drop half of jam by teaspoonfuls over filling; swirl gently with small knife or skewer, being careful not to overmix. Top with one third of filling; drop remaining jam by teaspoonfuls over filling and gently swirl jam. Spread remaining filling over top.

4. Place springform pan in roasting pan; fill roasting pan with hot water to come halfway up side of springform pan. Carefully place in oven. *Immediately reduce oven temperature to 350°F.* Bake about 1 hour 10 minutes or until top of cheesecake is lightly browned and center jiggles slightly. Remove cheesecake from roasting pan to wire rack; remove foil. Cool to room temperature. Cover and refrigerate 4 hours or overnight. Garnish with shaved white chocolate, whipped cream and raspberries.

24 crème-filled chocolate sandwich cookies, crushed into fine crumbs

3 tablespoons butter, melted

4 packages (8 ounces each) cream cheese, softened

1¼ cups sugar

½ cup sour cream

2 teaspoons vanilla

5 eggs, at room temperature

1 bar (4 ounces) white chocolate, chopped into ¼-inch pieces

¾ cup seedless raspberry jam, stirred

Shaved white chocolate

Whipped cream and fresh raspberries

MOCHA FUDGE BROWNIES

MAKES 16 BROWNIES

1. Preheat oven to 350°F. Grease 8-inch square baking pan.

2. Melt semisweet chocolate in top of double boiler over boiling water. Remove from heat; let cool slightly.

3. Beat sugar and butter in medium bowl with electric mixer at medium speed until light and fluffy. Add eggs, one at a time, beating until blended after each addition. Add chocolate, espresso powder and vanilla; beat until blended. Stir in flour, almonds and $1/2$ cup chocolate chips. Spread batter in prepared pan.

4. Bake 25 minutes or until set. Sprinkle with remaining $1/2$ cup chocolate chips. Let stand until melted; spread evenly over brownies. Cool completely in pan on wire rack. Cut into 2-inch squares.

2 ounces semisweet chocolate

$3/4$ cup sugar

$1/2$ cup (1 stick) butter, softened

2 eggs

2 teaspoons instant espresso powder

1 teaspoon vanilla

$1/2$ cup all-purpose flour

$1/2$ cup chopped toasted almonds

1 cup (6 ounces) milk chocolate chips, divided

SLOW-COOKER SLOW DAY

SIMPLE SLOW COOKER PORK ROAST

MAKES 6 SERVINGS

Layer potatoes, carrots and pork roast in slow cooker. (If necessary, cut roast in half to fit.) Add water. Cover; cook on LOW 6 to 8 hours or until vegetables are tender. Add peas during last hour of cooking. Season with salt and pepper.

4 to 5 new red potatoes, cut into bite-size pieces

4 carrots, cut into bite-size pieces

1 marinated pork loin roast (3 to 4 pounds)

$1/2$ cup water

1 package (10 ounces) frozen baby peas

Salt and black pepper

VEGETARIAN CHILI

MAKES 4 SERVINGS

1. Heat oil in large nonstick skillet over medium-high heat until hot. Add onion, bell pepper, jalapeño pepper and garlic; cook and stir 5 minutes or until tender.

2. Transfer onion mixture to slow cooker. Add remaining ingredients except sour cream and cheese; mix well. Cover; cook on LOW 4 to 5 hours.

3. Garnish with sour cream and cheese, if desired.

1 tablespoon vegetable oil

1 cup finely chopped onion

1 cup chopped red bell pepper

2 tablespoons minced jalapeño pepper*

1 clove garlic, minced

1 can (28 ounces) crushed tomatoes

1 can (about 15 ounces) black beans, rinsed and drained

1 can (about 15 ounces) chickpeas, rinsed and drained

1/2 cup corn

1/4 cup tomato paste

1 teaspoon sugar

1 teaspoon ground cumin

1 teaspoon dried basil

1 teaspoon chili powder

1/4 teaspoon black pepper

Sour cream and shredded Cheddar cheese (optional)

*Jalapeño peppers can sting and irritate the skin, so wear rubber gloves when handling peppers and do not touch your eyes.

ITALIAN COMBO SUBS

MAKES 6 SERVINGS

1. Heat oil in large skillet over medium-high heat. Brown beef strips in 2 batches. Place beef in slow cooker.

2. Brown sausage in same skillet, stirring to separate meat. Drain and discard fat. Add sausage to slow cooker.

3. Place bell pepper, onion and mushrooms, if desired, over meat in slow cooker. Season with salt and black pepper. Top with pasta sauce. Cover; cook on LOW 4 to 6 hours. Serve in bread.

SERVING SUGGESTION: Top with freshly grated Parmesan cheese.

1 tablespoon vegetable oil

1 pound boneless beef round steak, cut into thin strips

1 pound bulk Italian sausage

1 green bell pepper, cut into strips

1 medium onion, thinly sliced

1 can (4 ounces) sliced mushrooms, drained (optional)

Salt

Black pepper

1 jar (26 ounces) pasta sauce

2 loaves French bread, cut into 6-inch pieces and split

NO-FUSS MACARONI & CHEESE
MAKES 6 TO 8 SERVINGS

Combine macaroni, cheeses, salt and pepper in slow cooker. Pour milk over top. Cover; cook on LOW 2 to 3 hours, stirring after 20 to 30 minutes.

VARIATION: Stir in sliced hot dogs or vegetables near the end of cooking. Cover; cook until heated through.

NOTES: As with all macaroni and cheese dishes, the cheese sauce thickens and begins to dry out as it sits. If it becomes too dry, stir in a little extra milk. Do not cook longer than 4 hours.

This is a simple way to make macaroni and cheese without taking the time to boil water and cook noodles.

- 2 cups (about 8 ounces) uncooked elbow macaroni
- 4 ounces pasteurized process cheese product, cubed
- 1 cup (4 ounces) shredded mild Cheddar cheese
- 1/2 teaspoon salt
- 1/8 teaspoon black pepper
- 1 1/2 cups milk

CREAMY SLOW COOKER SEAFOOD CHOWDER

MAKES 8 TO 10 SERVINGS

1. Combine half-and-half, white potatoes, soup, hash brown potatoes, onion, butter, salt and pepper in 5- or 6-quart slow cooker. Mix well.

2. Cover; cook on LOW 3 to 4 hours.

3. Add oysters, clams and shrimp; stir gently. Cover; cook on LOW 30 to 45 minutes or until seafood is done.

1 quart (4 cups) half-and-half

2 cans (about 15 ounces each) whole white potatoes, rinsed, drained and cubed

2 cans ($10^3/_4$ ounces each) condensed cream of mushroom soup, undiluted

1 bag (16 ounces) frozen hash brown potatoes, thawed

1 medium onion, minced

$^1/_2$ cup (1 stick) butter, cubed

1 teaspoon salt

1 teaspoon black pepper

5 cans (about 8 ounces each) whole oysters, drained and rinsed

2 cans (about 6 ounces each) minced clams

2 cans (about 4 ounces each) cocktail shrimp, drained and rinsed

NANCY'S CHICKEN NOODLE SOUP

MAKES 4 SERVINGS

1. Combine all ingredients except noodles in 5-quart slow cooker.

2. Cover; cook on LOW 5 to 7 hours or on HIGH 3 to 4 hours. Stir in noodles 30 minutes before serving.

1 can (about 48 ounces) chicken broth

2 boneless skinless chicken breasts, cut into bite-size pieces

4 cups water

$2/3$ cup diced onion

$2/3$ cup diced celery

$2/3$ cup diced carrots

$2/3$ cup sliced mushrooms

$1/2$ cup frozen peas

4 cubes chicken bouillon

2 tablespoons butter

1 tablespoon dried parsley flakes

1 teaspoon salt

1 teaspoon ground cumin

1 teaspoon dried marjoram

1 teaspoon black pepper

2 cups cooked egg noodles

SHRIMP JAMBALAYA
MAKES 6 SERVINGS

1. Combine tomatoes with juice, onion, bell pepper, celery, garlic, parsley flakes, oregano, hot pepper sauce and thyme in slow cooker. Cover and cook on LOW 8 hours or on HIGH 4 hours.

2. Stir in shrimp. Cover and cook on LOW 20 minutes.

3. Meanwhile, prepare rice according to package directions, substituting broth for water. Serve jambalaya over hot cooked rice.

1 can (28 ounces) diced tomatoes, undrained

1 medium onion, chopped

1 medium red bell pepper, chopped

1 stalk celery, chopped

2 tablespoons minced garlic

2 teaspoons dried parsley flakes

2 teaspoons dried oregano

1 teaspoon hot pepper sauce

½ teaspoon dried thyme

2 pounds large cooked shrimp, peeled and deveined (with tails on)

2 cups uncooked instant rice

2 cups chicken broth

BEEF BRISKET DINNER

MAKES 8 TO 10 SERVINGS

1. Place brisket, potatoes, carrots, mushrooms, onion, celery, bouillon cubes, garlic, peppercorns and bay leaves in slow cooker. Add water to cover ingredients. Cover and cook on LOW 6 to 8 hours. Remove and discard bay leaves.

2. Remove brisket to cutting board. Slice meat across grain. Serve with vegetables.

1 beef brisket (4 pounds), cut in half

4 to 6 medium potatoes, cut into large chunks

6 carrots, cut into 1-inch pieces

8 ounces mushrooms, sliced

1/2 large onion, sliced

1 stalk celery, cut into 1-inch pieces

3 cubes beef bouillon

5 cloves garlic, crushed

1 teaspoon black peppercorns

2 whole bay leaves

Water

SLOW COOKER TURKEY BREAST

MAKES 4 TO 6 SERVINGS

1. Place turkey in slow cooker. Season with garlic powder, paprika and parsley flakes. Cover; cook on LOW 6 to 8 hours or until internal temperature reaches 170°F.

2. Remove turkey to cutting board; cover with foil and let stand 10 to 15 minutes before carving. (Internal temperature will rise 5° to 10°F during stand time.)

1 **boneless turkey breast (about 3 pounds)**

Garlic powder

Paprika

Dried parsley flakes

CHICKEN IN HONEY SAUCE
MAKES 4 TO 6 SERVINGS

1. Place chicken in slow cooker; season with salt and pepper.

2. Combine honey, soy sauce, ketchup, oil and garlic in medium bowl. Pour over chicken. Cover; cook on LOW 6 to 8 hours or on HIGH 3 to 4 hours.

3. Garnish with sesame seeds before serving.

4 to 6 boneless skinless chicken breasts

Salt and black pepper

2 cups honey

1 cup soy sauce

1/2 cup ketchup

1/4 cup oil

2 cloves garlic, minced

Sesame seeds (optional)

CORN CHIP CHILI
MAKES 6 SERVINGS

1. Coat inside of slow cooker with nonstick cooking spray.

2. Heat oil in large skillet over medium-high heat. Add onion, bell pepper, jalapeño pepper and garlic; cook and stir 2 minutes or until softened. Add beef; cook and stir 10 to 12 minutes or until beef is no longer pink and liquid has evaporated. Stir in green chiles; cook 1 minute. Remove beef mixture to slow cooker. Stir in tomatoes, chili powder, cumin and oregano.

3. Cover; cook on LOW 6 to 7 hours or on HIGH 3 to 3½ hours. Stir in the salt. Place corn chips evenly into serving bowls; top with chili. Sprinkle with cheese and green onions.

1 tablespoon olive oil

1 medium onion, chopped

1 medium red bell pepper, chopped

1 jalapeno pepper,* seeded and finely chopped

4 cloves garlic, minced

2 pounds ground beef

1 can (4 ounces) diced green chiles, drained

2 cans (about 14 ounces each) fire-roasted diced tomatoes

2 tablespoons chili powder

1½ teaspoons ground cumin

1½ teaspoons dried oregano

¾ teaspoon salt

3 cups corn chips

1 cup (4 ounces) shredded sharp Cheddar cheese

6 tablespoons chopped green onions

*Jalapeño peppers can sting and irritate the skin, so wear rubber gloves when handling peppers and do not touch your eyes.

SIMPLE SALMON WITH FRESH SALSA
MAKES 4 SERVINGS

1. Season salmon with ½ teaspoon salt, thyme and black pepper. Pour broth into slow cooker; add salmon. Cover; cook on LOW 3 hours.

2. Meanwhile, combine cucumber, bell pepper, radishes, tomatoes, cilantro, lime juice, onion and remaining ½ teaspoon salt in medium bowl. Cover; refrigerate until ready to serve.

3. To serve, place salmon on serving plates; top with salsa. Serve with green beans, if desired.

- 4 **salmon fillets (about 4 ounces** *each***), rinsed and patted dry**
- 1 **teaspoon salt, divided**
- ½ **teaspoon dried thyme, crumbled**
- ¼ **teaspoon black pepper**
- ½ **cup chicken broth**
- 1 **medium cucumber, peeled, seeded and chopped**
- ½ **large green bell pepper, chopped**
- ½ **cup finely chopped radishes**
- ½ **cup quartered grape tomatoes**
- ¼ **cup chopped fresh cilantro**
- 3 **tablespoons fresh lime juice**
- 2 **tablespoons finely chopped red onion**

  Hot cooked green beans (optional)

EASY BEEF STEW

MAKES 6 TO 8 SERVINGS

Combine all ingredients in slow cooker. Cover; cook on LOW 8 to 10 hours or until vegetables are tender.

$1\frac{1}{2}$ to 2 pounds beef stew meat

4 medium potatoes, cubed

4 cups baby carrots or 4 carrots, cut into $1\frac{1}{2}$-inch pieces

1 medium onion, cut into 8 pieces

2 cans (8 ounces each) tomato sauce

1 teaspoon salt

$\frac{1}{2}$ teaspoon black pepper

METRIC CONVERSION CHART

VOLUME MEASUREMENTS (dry)

$1/8$ teaspoon = 0.5 mL
$1/4$ teaspoon = 1 mL
$1/2$ teaspoon = 2 mL
$3/4$ teaspoon = 4 mL
1 teaspoon = 5 mL
1 tablespoon = 15 mL
2 tablespoons = 30 mL
$1/4$ cup = 60 mL
$1/3$ cup = 75 mL
$1/2$ cup = 125 mL
$2/3$ cup = 150 mL
$3/4$ cup = 175 mL
1 cup = 250 mL
2 cups = 1 pint = 500 mL
3 cups = 750 mL
4 cups = 1 quart = 1 L

VOLUME MEASUREMENTS (fluid)

1 fluid ounce (2 tablespoons) = 30 mL
4 fluid ounces ($1/2$ cup) = 125 mL
8 fluid ounces (1 cup) = 250 mL
12 fluid ounces ($1 1/2$ cups) = 375 mL
16 fluid ounces (2 cups) = 500 mL

WEIGHTS (mass)

$1/2$ ounce = 15 g
1 ounce = 30 g
3 ounces = 90 g
4 ounces = 120 g
8 ounces = 225 g
10 ounces = 285 g
12 ounces = 360 g
16 ounces = 1 pound = 450 g

DIMENSIONS

$1/16$ inch = 2 mm
$1/8$ inch = 3 mm
$1/4$ inch = 6 mm
$1/2$ inch = 1.5 cm
$3/4$ inch = 2 cm
1 inch = 2.5 cm

OVEN TEMPERATURES

250°F = 120°C
275°F = 140°C
300°F = 150°C
325°F = 160°C
350°F = 180°C
375°F = 190°C
400°F = 200°C
425°F = 220°C
450°F = 230°C

BAKING PAN SIZES

Utensil	Size in Inches/Quarts	Metric Volume	Size in Centimeters
Baking or Cake Pan (square or rectangular)	8×8×2	2 L	20×20×5
	9×9×2	2.5 L	23×23×5
	12×8×2	3 L	30×20×5
	13×9×2	3.5 L	33×23×5
Loaf Pan	8×4×3	1.5 L	20×10×7
	9×5×3	2 L	23×13×7
Round Layer Cake Pan	8×1½	1.2 L	20×4
	9×1½	1.5 L	23×4
Pie Plate	8×1¼	750 mL	20×3
	9×1¼	1 L	23×3
Baking Dish or Casserole	1 quart	1 L	—
	1½ quart	1.5 L	—
	2 quart	2 L	—